TOUCHSTONE

FULL CONTACT

MICHAEL MCCARTHY
JEANNE MCCARTEN
HELEN SANDIFORD

2A

STUDENT'S BOOK

CAMBRIDGE
UNIVERSITY PRESS

CAMBRIDGE UNIVERSITY PRESS
Cambridge, New York, Melbourne, Madrid, Cape Town,
Singapore, São Paulo, Delhi, Mexico City

Cambridge University Press
32 Avenue of the Americas, New York, NY 10013-2473, USA

www.cambridge.org
Information on this title: www.cambridge.org/9780521757904

First published 2008
7th printing 2013

Printed in Lima, Peru, by Empresa Editora El Comercio S.A.

A catalog record for this publication is available from the British Library.

ISBN 978-0-521-75790-4 paperback

Art direction, book design, photo research, and layout services: Adventure House, NYC
and TSI Graphics, Illinois
Audio production: Full House, NYC
CD-ROM / DVD production: a/t media services, inc., New Hampshire

Authors' acknowledgments

Touchstone has benefited from extensive development research. The authors and publishers would like to extend their particular thanks to the following reviewers, consultants, and piloters for their valuable insights and suggestions.

Reviewers and consultants:

Thomas Job Lane and Marilia de M. Zanella from **Associação Alumni**, São Paulo, Brazil; Simon Banha from **Phil Young's English School**, Curitiba, Brazil; Katy Cox from **Casa Thomas Jefferson**, Brasilia, Brazil; Rodrigo Santana from **CCBEU**, Goiânia, Brazil; Cristina Asperti, Nancy H. Lake, and Airton Pretini Junior from **CEL LEP**, São Paulo, Brazil; Sonia Cury from **Centro Britânico**, São Paulo, Brazil; Daniela Alves Meyer from **IBEU**, Rio de Janeiro, Brazil; Ayeska Farias from **Mai English**, Belo Horizonte, Brazil; Solange Cassiolato from **LTC**, São Paulo, Brazil; Fernando Prestes Maia from **Polidiomas**, São Paulo, Brazil; Chris Ritchie and Debora Schisler from **Seven Idiomas**, São Paulo, Brazil; Maria Teresa Maiztegui and Joacyr de Oliveira from **União Cultural EEUU**, São Paulo, Brazil; Sakae Onoda from **Chiba University of Commerce**, Ichikawa, Japan; James Boyd and Ann Conlon from **ECC Foreign Language Institute**, Osaka, Japan; Catherine Chamier from **ELEC**, Tokyo, Japan; Janaka Williams, Japan; David Aline from **Kanagawa University**, Yokohama, Japan; Brian Long from **Kyoto University of Foreign Studies**, Kyoto, Japan; Alistair Home and Brian Quinn from **Kyushu University**, Fukuoka, Japan; Rafael Dovale from **Matsushita Electric Industrial Co., Ltd.**, Osaka, Japan; Bill Acton, Michael Herriman, Bruce Monk, and Alan Thomson from **Nagoya University of Commerce**, Nisshin, Japan; Alan Bessette from **Poole Gakuin University**, Osaka, Japan; Brian Collins from **Sundai Foreign Language Institute, Tokyo College of Music**, Tokyo, Japan; Todd Odgers from **The Tokyo Center for Language and Culture**, Tokyo, Japan; Jion Hanagata from **Tokyo Foreign Language College**, Tokyo, Japan; Peter Collins and Charlene Mills from **Tokai University**, Hiratsuka, Japan; David Stewart from **Tokyo Institute of Technology**, Tokyo, Japan; Alberto Peto Villalobos from **Cenlex Santo Tomás**, Mexico City, Mexico; Diana Jones and Carlos Lizarraga from **Instituto Angloamericano**, Mexico City, Mexico; Raúl Mar and María Teresa Monroy from **Universidad de Cuautitlán Izcalli**, Mexico City, Mexico; JoAnn Miller from **Universidad del Valle de México**, Mexico City, Mexico; Orlando Carranza from **ICPNA**, Peru; Sister Melanie Bair and Jihyeon Jeon from **The Catholic University of Korea**, Seoul, South Korea; Peter E. Nelson from **Chung-Ang University**, Seoul, South Korea; Joseph Schouweiler from **Dongguk University**, Seoul, South Korea; Michael Brazil and Sean Witty from **Gwangwoon University**, Seoul, South Korea; Kelly Martin and Larry Michienzi from **Hankook FLS University**, Seoul, South Korea; Scott Duerstock and Jane Miller from **Konkuk University**, Seoul, South Korea; Athena Pichay from **Korea University**, Seoul, South Korea; Lane Darnell Bahl, Susan Caesar, and Aaron Hughes from **Korea University**, Seoul, South Korea; Farzana Hyland and Stephen van Vlack from **Sookmyung Women's University**, Seoul, South Korea; Hae-Young Kim, Terry Nelson, and Ron Schafrick from **Sungkyunkwan University**, Seoul, South Korea; Mary Chen and Michelle S. M. Fan from **Chinese Cultural University**, Taipei, Taiwan; Joseph Sorell from **Christ's College**, Taipei, Taiwan; Dan Aldridge and Brian Kleinsmith from **ELSI**, Taipei, Taiwan; Ching-Shyang Anna Chien and Duen-Yeh Charles Chang from **Hsin Wu Institute of Technology**, Taipei, Taiwan; Timothy Hogan, Andrew Rooney, and Dawn Young from **Language Training and Testing Center**, Taipei, Taiwan; Jen Mei Hsu and Yu-hwei Eunice Shih from **National Taiwan Normal University**, Taipei, Taiwan; Roma Starczewska and Su-Wei Wang from **PQ3R Taipei Language and Computer Center**, Taipei, Taiwan; Elaine Paris from **Shih Chien University**, Taipei, Taiwan; Jennifer Castello from **Cañada College**, Redwood City, California, USA; Dennis Johnson, Gregory Keech, and Penny Larson from **City College of San Francisco – Institute for International Students**, San Francisco, California, USA; Ditra Henry from **College of Lake County**, Gray's Lake, Illinois, USA; Madeleine Murphy from **College of San Mateo**, San Mateo, California, USA; Ben Yoder from **Harper College**, Palatine, Illinois, USA; Christine Aguila, John Lanier, Armando Mata, and Ellen Sellergren from **Lakeview Learning Center**, Chicago, Illinois, USA; Ellen Gomez from **Laney College**, Oakland, California, USA; Brian White from **Northeastern Illinois University**, Chicago, Illinois, USA; Randi Reppen from **Northern Arizona University**, Flagstaff, Arizona, USA; Janine Gluud from **San Francisco State University – College of Extended Learning**, San Francisco, California, USA; Peg Sarosy from **San Francisco State University – American Language Institute**, San Francisco, California, USA; David Mitchell from **UC Berkley Extension, ELP – English Language Program**, San Francisco, California, USA; Eileen Censotti, Kim Knutson, Dave Onufrock, Marnie Ramker, and Jerry Stanfield from **University of Illinois at Chicago – Tutorium in Intensive English**, Chicago, Illinois, USA; Johnnie Johnson Hafernik from **University of San Francisco, ESL Program**, San Francisco, California, USA; Judy Friedman from **New York Institute of Technology**, New York, New York, USA; Sheila Hackner from **St. John's University**, New York, New York, USA; Joan Lesikin from **William Paterson University**, Wayne, New Jersey, USA; Linda Pelc from **LaGuardia Community College**, Long Island City, New York, USA; Tamara Plotnick from **Pace University**, New York, USA; Lenore Rosenbluth from **Montclair State University**, Montclair, New Jersey, USA; Suzanne Seidel from **Nassau Community College**, Garden City, New York, USA; Debbie Un from **New York University, New School**, and **LaGuardia Community College**, New York, New York, USA; Cynthia Wiseman from **Hunter College**, New York, New York, USA; Aaron Lawson from **Cornell University**, Ithaca, New York, USA, for his help in corpus research; Belkis Yanes from **CTC Belo Monte**, Caracas, Venezuela; Victoria García from **English World**, Caracas, Venezuela; Kevin Bandy from **LT Language Teaching Services**, Caracas, Venezuela; Ivonne Quintero from **PDVSA**, Caracas, Venezuela.

Piloters:

Daniela Jorge from **ELFE Idiomas**, São Paulo, Brazil; Eloisa Marchesi Oliveira from **ETE Professor Camargo Aranha**, São Paulo, Brazil; Marilena Wanderley Pessoa from **IBEU**, Rio de Janeiro, Brazil; Marcia Lotaif from **LTC**, São Paulo, Brazil; Mirlei Valenzi from **USP English on Campus**, São Paulo, Brazil; Jelena Johanovic from **YEP International**, São Paulo, Brazil; James Steinman from **Osaka International College for Women**, Moriguchi, Japan; Brad Visgatis from **Osaka International University for Women**, Moriguchi, Japan; William Figoni from **Osaka Institute of Technology**, Osaka, Japan; Terry O'Brien from **Otani Women's University**, Tondabayashi, Japan; Gregory Kennerly from **YMCA Language Center** piloted at **Hankyu SHS**, Osaka, Japan; Daniel Alejandro Ramos and Salvador Enríquez Castaneda from **Instituto Cultural Mexicano-Norteamericano de Jalisco**, Guadalajara, Mexico; Patricia Robinson and Melida Valdes from **Universidad de Guadalajara**, Guadalajara, Mexico.

We would also like to thank the people who arranged recordings: Debbie Berktold, Bobbie Gore, Bill Kohler, Aaron Lawson, Terri Massin, Traci Suiter, Bryan Swan, and the many people who agreed to be recorded.

The authors would also like to thank the **editorial** and **production** team:
Sue Aldcorn, Eleanor K. Barnes, Janet Battiste, Sylvia P. Bloch, David Bohlke, Karen Brock, Jeff Chen, Sylvia Dare, Karen Davy, Deborah Goldblatt, Paul Heacock, Louisa Hellegers, Cindee Howard, Eliza Jensen, Lesley Koustaff, Heather McCarron, Lise R. Minovitz, Diana Nam, Kathy Niemczyk, Sandra Pike, Bill Preston, Janet Raskin, Mary Sandre, Tamar Savir, Susannah Sodergren, Shelagh Speers, Kayo Taguchi, Mary Vaughn, Jennifer Wilkin, and all the design and production team at Adventure House.

And these Cambridge University Press **staff** and **advisors**:
Yumiko Akeba, Jim Anderson, Kanako Aoki, Mary Louise Baez, Carlos Barbisan, Alexandre Canizares, Cruz Castro, Kathleen Corley, Kate Cory-Wright, Riitta da Costa, Peter Davison, Elizabeth Fuzikava, Steven Golden, Yuri Hara, Catherine Higham, Gareth Knight, João Madureira, Andy Martin, Alejandro Martínez, Nigel McQuitty, Carine Mitchell, Mark O'Neil, Rebecca Ou, Antonio Puente, Colin Reublinger, Andrew Robinson, Dan Schulte, Kumiko Sekioka, Catherine Shih, Howard Siegelman, Ivan Sorrentino, Ian Sutherland, Alcione Tavares, Koen Van Landeghem, Sergio Varela, and Ellen Zlotnick.

In addition, the authors would like to thank Colin Hayes and Jeremy Mynott for making the project possible in the first place. Most of all, very special thanks are due to Mary Vaughn for her dedication, support, and professionalism. Helen Sandiford would like to thank her family and especially her husband, Bryan Swan, for his support and love.

Welcome to Touchstone!

We created the **Touchstone** series with the help of the *Cambridge International Corpus* of North American English. The corpus is a large database of language from everyday conversations, radio and television broadcasts, and newspapers and books.

Using computer software, we analyze the corpus to find out how people actually use English. We use the corpus as a "touchstone" to make sure that each lesson teaches you authentic and useful language. The corpus helps us choose and explain the grammar, vocabulary, and conversation strategies you need to communicate successfully in English.

Touchstone makes learning English fun. It gives you many different opportunities to interact with your classmates. You can exchange personal information, take class surveys, role-play situations, play games, and discuss topics of personal interest. Using **Touchstone**, you can develop confidence in your ability to understand real-life English and to express yourself clearly and effectively in everyday situations.

We hope you enjoy using **Touchstone** and wish you every success with your English classes.

Michael McCarthy
Jeanne McCarten
Helen Sandiford

Unit features

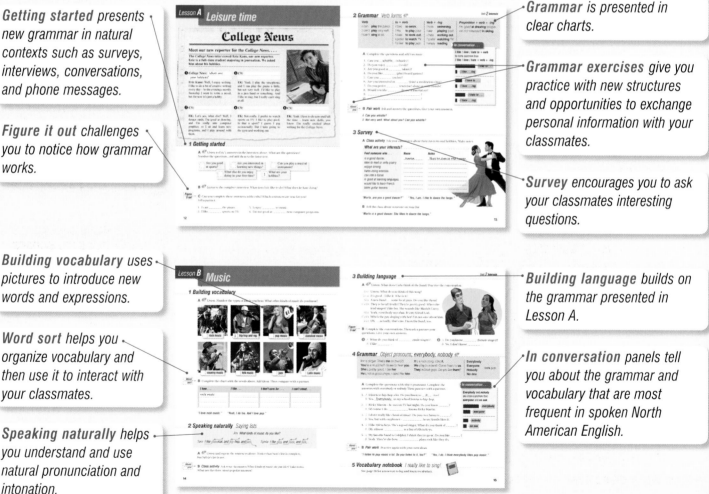

Getting started presents new grammar in natural contexts such as surveys, interviews, conversations, and phone messages.

Figure it out challenges you to notice how grammar works.

Building vocabulary uses pictures to introduce new words and expressions.

Word sort helps you organize vocabulary and then use it to interact with your classmates.

Speaking naturally helps you understand and use natural pronunciation and intonation.

Grammar is presented in clear charts.

Grammar exercises give you practice with new structures and opportunities to exchange personal information with your classmates.

Survey encourages you to ask your classmates interesting questions.

Building language builds on the grammar presented in Lesson A.

In conversation panels tell you about the grammar and vocabulary that are most frequent in spoken North American English.

Conversation strategy helps you "manage" conversations better. In this lesson, you learn how to say **no** in a friendly way. The strategies are based on examples from the corpus.

Reading has interesting texts from newspapers, magazines, and the Internet. The activities help you develop reading skills.

Vocabulary notebook is a page of fun activities to help you organize and write down vocabulary.

On your own is a practical task to help you learn vocabulary outside of class.

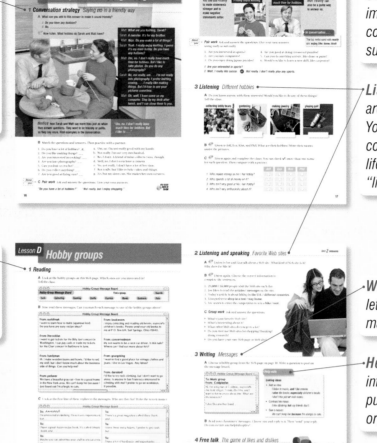

Strategy plus teaches important expressions for conversation management, such as **really** and **not really**.

Listening and speaking skills are often practiced together. You listen to a variety of conversations based on real-life language. Tasks include "listen and react" activities.

Writing tasks include e-mails, letters, short articles, and material for Web pages.

Help notes give you information on things like punctuation, linking ideas, and organizing information.

Fun facts from the corpus tell you the most frequent words and expressions for different topics.

Free talk helps you engage in free conversation with your classmates.

Other features

A **Touchstone checkpoint** after every three units reviews grammar, vocabulary, and conversation strategies.

A **Self-study Audio CD/ CD-ROM** gives you more practice with listening, speaking, and vocabulary building.

The **Class Audio Program** presents the conversations and listening activities in natural, lively English.

The **Workbook** gives you language practice and extra reading and writing activities. **Progress checks** help you assess your progress.

Touchstone *Level 2A Scope and sequence*

	Functions / Topics	Grammar	Vocabulary	Conversation strategies	Pronunciation
Unit 1 **Making friends** pages 1–10	• Ask questions to get to know your classmates • Talk about yourself, your family, and your favorite things • Show you have something in common	• Review of simple present and present of *be* in questions and statements • Responses with *too* and *either*	• Review of types of TV shows, clothes, food, and weekend activities	• Start a conversation with someone you don't know • Use *actually* to give or "correct" information	• Stress and intonation in questions and answers
Unit 2 **Interests** pages 11–20	• Ask about people's interests and hobbies • Talk about your interests, hobbies, and taste in music	• Verb forms after *can / can't, love, like,* etc., and prepositions • Object pronouns • *Everybody, everyone, nobody,* and *no one*	• Interests and hobbies • Types of music	• Say *no* in a friendly way • Use *really* and *not really* to make statements stronger or softer	• Saying lists
Unit 3 **Health** pages 21–30	• Talk about how to stay healthy • Describe common health problems • Talk about what you do when you have a health problem	• Simple present and present continuous • Joining clauses with *if* and *when*	• Ways to stay healthy • Common health problems • Common remedies	• Encourage people to say more to keep a conversation going • Show surprise	• Contrasts

Touchstone checkpoint Units 1–3   pages 31–32

	Functions / Topics	Grammar	Vocabulary	Conversation strategies	Pronunciation
Unit 4 **Celebrations** pages 33–42	• Talk about birthdays, celebrations, and favorite holidays • Describe how you celebrate special days • Talk about plans and predictions	• Future with *going to* • Indirect objects • Indirect object pronouns • Present continuous for the future	• Months of the year • Days of the month • Special days, celebrations, and holidays • Things people do to celebrate special days	• Use "vague" expressions like *and everything* • Give "vague" responses like *I don't know* and *Maybe* when you're not sure	• Reduction of *going to*
Unit 5 **Growing up** pages 43–52	• Talk about life events and memories of growing up • Talk about school and your teenage years	• Review of simple past in questions and statements • *be born* • General and specific use of determiners	• Time expressions for the past • Saying years • School subjects	• Correct things you say with expressions like *Well; Actually;* and *No, wait* • Use *I mean* to correct yourself when you say the wrong word or name	• Reduction of *did you*
Unit 6 **Around town** pages 53–62	• Ask and answer questions about places in a town • Give directions • Offer help and ask for directions • Talk about stores and favorite places in your town • Recommend places in your neighborhood	• *Is there?* and *Are there?* • Pronouns *one* and *some* • Offers and requests with *Can* and *Could*	• Places in town • Location expressions • Expressions for asking and giving directions	• Repeat key words to check information • Use "checking" expressions to check information • Use "echo" questions to check information	• Word stress in compound nouns

Touchstone checkpoint Units 4–6   pages 63–64

Listening	Reading	Writing	Vocabulary notebook	Free talk
What's the question? • Listen to answers and match them with questions *Sally's party* • Listen to responses and match them to conversation starters; then listen for more information	*How to improve your conversation skills* • A magazine article giving advice	• Write an article giving advice on how to improve something • Review of punctuation	*Webs of words* • Use word webs to organize new vocabulary	*Me too!* • Class activity: Ask questions to find classmates who have things in common with you
Different hobbies • Match four conversations about hobbies with photos, and fill in a chart *Favorite Web sites* • Listen for details as two people talk about a Web site	• A Web page for hobby groups	• Write an e-mail message to one of the hobby groups on the Web page • Link ideas with *and, also, especially, or, but,* and *because*	*I really like to sing!* • Link new words together in word "chains"	*The game of likes and dislikes* • Group work: Each person fills out a chart. Then groups compare answers and score points for finding things in common.
Unhealthy habits • Predict what four people will say about their bad habits, and then listen for the exact words *Time to chill out* • Match four conversations about relaxing with photos, and listen for details	• A leaflet about stress from the Department of Health	• Write a question asking advice about a health problem, and write replies to your classmates' questions • Commas after *if* and *when* clauses	*Under the weather* • Write down words you can use with a new word or expression	*Are you taking care of your health?* • Pair work: Answer a health questionnaire with your partner, and figure out your partner's score

*Touchstone **checkpoint** Units 1–3   pages 31–32*

Listening	Reading	Writing	Vocabulary notebook	Free talk
Celebrations around the world • Listen to people talk about two festivals, and answer questions *Congratulations!* • Listen for details in two conversations about invitations, and fill in the blanks	*Time to celebrate!* • An article about traditions in different countries	• Write an invitation to a special event, and add a personal note • Formal and informal ways to begin and end a note or letter	*Calendars* • Write new vocabulary about special days and celebrations on a calendar	*A new celebration* • Group work: Create a new special day or festival, and talk about it with other groups
I don't remember exactly . . . • Listen for corrections people make as they talk about childhood memories *A long time ago* • Listen for details as a man talks about his teenage years	*An interview with . . . Jennifer Wilkin* • An interview with a woman who talks about her teenage years	• Write interview questions to ask a classmate about when he or she was younger, and reply to a classmate's questions • Link ideas with *except (for)* and *apart from*	*I hated math!* • Group new vocabulary in different ways	*In the past* • Class activity: Ask your classmates questions about their childhood, and take notes
Finding your way around • Match four sets of directions with the destinations by following the map *Tourist information* • Listen to conversations at a tourist-information desk, and predict what each person says next to check the information	*A walking tour of San Francisco's Chinatown* • Pages from a walking-tour guide	• Write a guide for a walking tour of your city or town • Expressions for giving directions	*Which way?* • Draw and label a map to remember directions	*Summer fun* • Pair work: Ask and answer questions about two different resorts, and choose one for a vacation

*Touchstone **checkpoint** Units 4–6   pages 63–64*

Getting help

How do you say "_____" in English?

I'm sorry. What did you say?

How do you say this word?

What do we have to do?

I don't understand. What do you mean?

Do you mean _____ ?

Can you spell "_____" for me, please?

Working with a partner

Whose turn is it now?

It's my / your turn.

Who goes first, A or B?

A does. That's me / you.

This time we change roles.

OK. I'll start.

Are we done?

Yes, I think so. Let's try it again.

Let's compare answers.

OK. What do you have for number 1?

Do you have _____ for number 3?

No, I have _____ . Let's check again.

Do you understand this sentence?

Yeah. It means "_____ ."

Making friends

In Unit 1, you learn how to . . .

- use the simple present and present of *be* (review).
- give responses with *too* and *either*.
- talk about yourself, your family, and your favorite things.
- start a conversation with someone you don't know.
- use *actually* to give or "correct" information.

2

4

1

3

Before you begin . . .

Imagine you want to get to know someone.
What questions can you ask about each topic?

- home and family
- studies
- work
- free time

Getting to know you

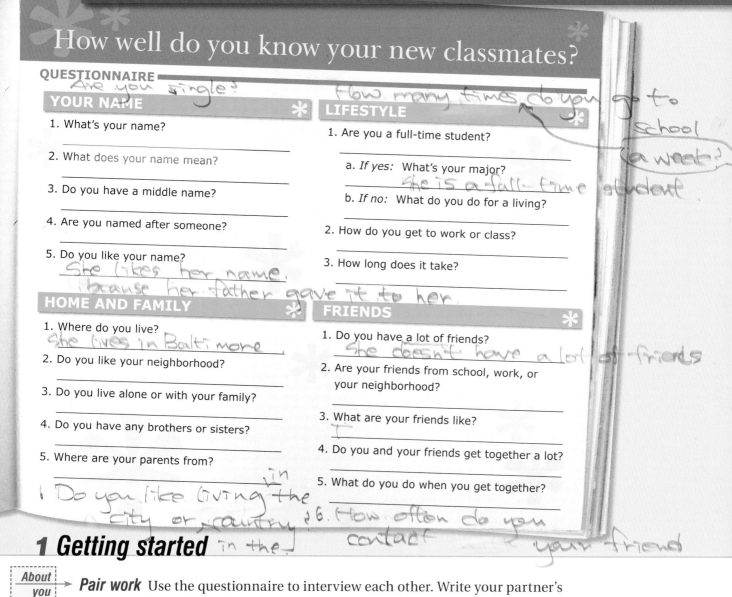

How well do you know your new classmates?

QUESTIONNAIRE

Are you single?

YOUR NAME ✱
1. What's your name?
2. What does your name mean?
3. Do you have a middle name?
4. Are you named after someone?
5. Do you like your name?

She likes her name, because her father gave it to her.

HOME AND FAMILY ✱
1. Where do you live?

She lives in Baltimore

2. Do you like your neighborhood?
3. Do you live alone or with your family?
4. Do you have any brothers or sisters?
5. Where are your parents from?

Do you like living the city or country? in the

LIFESTYLE ✱

How many times do you go to school a week?

1. Are you a full-time student?
   a. *If yes:* What's your major?

   She is a full-time student.

   b. *If no:* What do you do for a living?
2. How do you get to work or class?
3. How long does it take?

FRIENDS ✱
1. Do you have a lot of friends?

She doesn't have a lot of friends

2. Are your friends from school, work, or your neighborhood?
3. What are your friends like?
4. Do you and your friends get together a lot?
5. What do you do when you get together?

6. How often do you contact your friend

1 Getting started

> **About you** **Pair work** Use the questionnaire to interview each other. Write your partner's answers. Then tell the class one interesting thing about your partner.
>
> *"Marcella has seven brothers and sisters."*

[contact (my friend)
[connect with (my friend)

2 Speaking naturally *Stress and intonation*

Do you have a nickname?   Are you from a big family?   What do you do for fun?

Yes. People call me Jimmy.   Yes. I have four sisters.   I go to the movies.

A Listen and repeat the questions and answers above. Notice the stress on the important content word. Notice how the voice rises, or rises and then falls, on the stressed word.

> **About you** **B Pair work** Ask and answer the questions. Give your own answers.

3 **Grammar** *Simple present and present of* **be** *(review)*

Are you from a big family?
Yes, I **am**. I'm one of six children.
No, I'**m not**. There are only two of us.

Are you and your friends full-time students?
Yes, we **are**. We're English majors.
No, we'**re not**. We're part-time students.

What'**s** your name? **Is** it Leo?
Yes, it **is**. My name'**s** Leo Green.
No, it'**s not**. My name **isn't** Leo. It'**s** Joe.

Where **are** your parents from? **Are** they from Peru?
Yes, they **are**. They'**re** from Lima.
No, they'**re not**. My parents **aren't** from Peru.

Do you **have** any brothers and sisters?
Yes, I **do**. I have a brother.
No, I **don't**. I'm an only child.

Do you and your friends **get** together a lot?
Yes, we **do**. We go out all the time.
No, we **don't**. We don't have time.

What **does** your brother **do**? **Does** he **go** to college?
Yes, he **does**. He **goes** to the same college as me.
No, he **doesn't**. He **works** at a bank.

Where **do** your parents **live**? **Do** they **live** nearby?
Yes, they **do**. They **live** near here.
No, they **don't**. They **don't live** around here.

A Think of a possible question for each answer. Compare with a partner.

[handwritten: nights?]
[handwritten: do on Friday]

1. *A* _What's your favorite color?_
   B Red.

2. *A* _Are you from a big family?_
   B No, I'm not. I have one sister.

3. *A* _Do you drive_ ?
   B No, I don't. I don't drive.

4. *A* _Where does he work?_
   B He works in a store.

5. *A* _What do you and your friend?_
   B We usually go out to dinner or see a movie.

6. *A* _Do they spend a lot of time_ *[exercising]*
   B No, they don't. They don't have time.

7. *A* _Are you a morning person?_
   B No, I hate mornings. I'm not a morning person.

8. *A* _Do you have a job?_
   B Well, I have a part-time job. I work Saturdays.

About you

B *Pair work* Ask and answer the questions. Give your own answers.

[handwritten: easy to say ⟷ difficult to say]

4 *Listening and speaking* What's the question?

A Listen to Tom's answers to these questions. Number the questions 1 to 6.

☐ "Do you have any pets?"

1 "What's your favorite name?" *[handwritten: season]*

☐ "Who's your favorite actor?"

☐ "What do you do on weeknights?"

☐ "When do you spend time with your family?"

☐ "Do you go out a lot on weekends?"

[handwritten: hour.   every sunday]

About you

B *Group work* Choose one of the questions, and tell the group your answer.
Then answer a follow-up question from each person in your group.

"My favorite name is Jennifer." ➡

"How do you spell that?"
"Why do you like that name?"
"Do you have a favorite boy's name?"

1 Building language

A 🔘 Listen. What do these friends have in common? Practice the conversations.

❶

A Dogs are so noisy, and they always wreck things. I'm just not an animal lover, I guess.
B Well, I'm not either. I'm allergic to dogs and cats.

❷

A I don't watch much television.
B No, I don't either.
A I mean, I watch pro football.
B Yeah, I do too. But that's about it.

❸

A I love shopping. I can shop for hours! Too bad I can't afford anything new.
B I know. I can't either. I'm broke.
A Yeah, I am too.

Figure it out ➡ **B** Can you complete the answers? Use the conversations above to help you.

❶ A I'm not a football fan.
    B I'm _____ either.

❷ A I love shopping.
    B I _____ too.

❸ A I can't have a pet.
    B I can't _____ .

2 Grammar *Responses with too and either* 🔘

I'm allergic to cats.	**I watch** pro football.	**I can** shop for hours!
I **am too**.	I **do too**.	I **can too**.
I'm not an animal lover.	**I don't** watch much television.	**I can't** afford anything new.
I'm not either.	**I don't either**.	**I can't either**.

*People also respond with **Me too** and **Me neither** (or **Me either**).*

A Respond to these statements using *too* or *either*. Then practice with a partner.

1. I watch a lot of TV.   *I do too.*
2. I'm allergic to some foods.
3. I can't afford a new car.
4. I'm not a sports fan.
5. I don't have a pet.
6. I can shop all day.

In conversation . . .

People actually say **Me either** more often than **Me neither**.

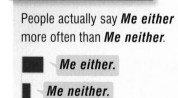

Me either.

Me neither.

About you ➡ **B** *Pair work* Student A: Make the statements above true for you.
Student B: Give your own responses.

"I don't watch a lot of TV."   *"I don't either."* **or** *"Really? I watch TV all the time."*

3 Building vocabulary

A Brainstorm! How many words can you think of for each topic? Make a class list.

TV shows   clothes   food   weekend activities

Word sort

B Complete the chart with your favorites from the class list. Compare with a partner. Then tell the class what you and your partner have in common.

My favorite . . .

weekend activities	TV shows	food	clothes
sleep late			

A *I sleep late on the weekends.*
B *I do too.*

➡️ *"We both sleep late on the weekends."*

About you

C Complete the sentences with your likes and dislikes. Then tell your classmates your sentences. Find someone who feels the same way.

Who has the same tastes as you?

My likes and dislikes	Classmate who feels the same way
1. *I can't stand* _____ . (type of TV show)	_____
2. *I often* _____ . (weekend activity)	_____
3. *I love to wear* _____ . (item of clothing)	_____
4. *I don't like* _____ *too much.* (color)	_____
5. *I'm not a* _____ *fan.* (sport)	_____
6. *I hate* _____ . (type of food)	_____

"I can't stand soap operas. How about you?"   *"I can't either."*

4 Vocabulary notebook   *Webs of words*

See page 10 for a new way to log and learn vocabulary.

Do you come here a lot?

1 Conversation strategy *Starting a conversation*

A Which topics can you talk about when you meet someone for the first time? Check (✓) the boxes below.

- ☐ your salary
- ☐ your health
- ☐ your family
- ☐ where you live
- ☐ the weather
- ☐ your problems
- ☐ someone's appearance
- ☐ things you see around you

Now listen. What are Eve and Chris talking about?

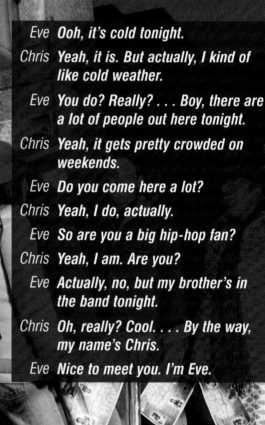

Eve	Ooh, it's cold tonight.
Chris	Yeah, it is. But actually, I kind of like cold weather.
Eve	You do? Really? . . . Boy, there are a lot of people out here tonight.
Chris	Yeah, it gets pretty crowded on weekends.
Eve	Do you come here a lot?
Chris	Yeah, I do, actually.
Eve	So are you a big hip-hop fan?
Chris	Yeah, I am. Are you?
Eve	Actually, no, but my brother's in the band tonight.
Chris	Oh, really? Cool. . . . By the way, my name's Chris.
Eve	Nice to meet you. I'm Eve.

Notice how Eve starts a conversation with a stranger. She talks about the things around them, like the weather and the club, and asks general questions. Find examples in the conversation.

"Ooh, it's cold tonight."
"Do you come here a lot?"

B *Pair work* Think of a way to start a conversation for each situation. Compare with a partner. Then role-play the situations. Continue each conversation as long as you can.

1. You meet someone new at a party. The food is really good.   *"This food is delicious!"*
2. It's a very hot day. You're just arriving at a new class.
3. You're in a long line at a movie theater. It's a cold day.
4. You're working out at a new gym. The music is very loud.
5. You're in a new English class. You meet someone during the break.
6. You're at the bus stop on a beautiful day. Someone arrives and smiles at you.

SELF-STUDY
AUDIO CD
CD-ROM

2 Strategy plus *Actually*

You can use *actually* **to give new or surprising information.**

> Do you come here a lot?

> Yeah, I do, actually.

You can also use *actually* **to "correct" things people say or think.**

A So, you're American?
B Well, *actually*, I'm from Canada.

> **In conversation . . .**
>
> *Actually* is one of the top 200 words.

A Match each conversation starter with a response. Then practice with a partner.

1. I like your jacket. _d_
2. Do you come here by bus? _____
3. Is that your newspaper? _____
4. Do you like this class? _____
5. Do you live around here? _____
6. Boy, it's warm in here. _____

a. Actually, I feel a bit cold.
b. Yeah. I actually look forward to it.
c. No, I walk, actually. It takes an hour.
d. Thanks. It's from Peru, actually.
e. Um . . . actually, no, it's not. Go ahead and take it.
f. Yes, right around the corner, actually.

About you → **B** *Pair work* Start conversations using the ideas above. Use *actually* in your responses if you need to.

"I like your watch."   *"Thanks. It was my grandfather's, actually."*

3 Listening *Sally's party*

A 💿 Listen to six people talk at Sally's party. Which conversation starters are the people responding to? Number the sentences.

☐ *"Gosh, the music really is loud, huh?"*

☐ *"Mmm. The food looks good."*

☐ *"This is a great party."*

☐ *"Are you a friend of Sally's?"*

[1] *"Is it me, or is it really hot in here?"*

☐ *"I don't really know anyone here. Do you?"*

B 💿 Now listen to the complete conversations. Check your answers. What do you find out about Sally?

4 Free talk *Me too!*

See **Free talk 1** at the back of the book for more speaking practice.

1 Reading

A Which of these are good suggestions for social conversations?
Check (✓) the boxes. Then tell the class.

☐ Don't look at the other person.
☐ Keep quiet when the other person is talking.
☐ Ask questions that start with *what, where, how,* or *when.*

☐ Have some good topics to discuss.
☐ Talk about yourself a lot.

B Read the magazine article. What does it say about the suggestions above?
Do you agree with all of the ideas in the article?

How to improve your conversation skills

Do you like to meet new people? Do you like to talk, or are you shy? Whatever your answers, this guide can help you improve your conversation skills.

1 Have some topics ready to start a conversation. Say something about the weather or the place you're in. Talk about the weekend – we all have something to say about weekends!

2 Make the conversation interesting. Know about events in the news. Read restaurant and movie reviews. Find out about the current music scene or what's new in fashion or sports.

3 Be a good listener. Keep eye contact and say, "Yes," "Hmm," "Uh-huh," "Right," and "I know." And say, "Really? That's interesting." It encourages people to talk.

4 Don't be boring. Don't just say, "Yes" or "No" when you answer a question. Give some interesting information, too.

5 Don't talk all the time. Ask, "How about you?" and show you are interested in the other person, too. People love to talk about themselves!

6 Ask information questions. Ask questions like "What do you do in your free time?" or "What kind of food do you like?" Use follow-up questions to keep the conversation going. But don't ask too many questions – it's not an interrogation!

7 Be positive. Negative comments can sound rude. And if you don't want to answer a personal question, simply say, "Oh, I'm not sure I can answer that," or "I'd rather not say."

8 Smile! Everyone loves a smile. Just be relaxed, smile, and be yourself.

C Look at the article again. Find these things. Then compare with a partner.

1. an interesting topic of conversation
2. an example of an information question
3. a suggestion you would like to try
4. a question to show you're interested in the other person
5. something you can say to show you're listening
6. something to say if someone asks you a difficult question

2 Speaking and writing *How to improve your . . .*

A *Pair work* Brainstorm ideas for each topic, and make notes.

How to improve your social life
Go out.   Be friendly.
Take up a sport or hobby.

How to improve your English

How to improve your study skills

B Choose one of the topics above, and use your ideas to write a short magazine article like the example below.

Document 1

How to Improve Your Social Life

Do you feel lonely? Do you want to make new friends? Here are some ideas to help you.

1. **Be friendly.** Talk to people at school and work. Smile and say, "Hi. How are you?" to new people.

2. **Go out a lot.** Go to coffee shops, bookstores, clubs, and sports events. Try to start conversations with people around you.

> **Help note**

Punctuation

- Use a CAPITAL letter to start a sentence.
- Use a comma (**,**) before quotation marks (**" "**) and in lists.
- Use a period (**.**) at the end of a statement and a question mark (**?**) at the end of a question.

3 Talk about it *Friendly conversation*

Group work Discuss the questions. Find out about your classmates' conversation styles.

▶ Do you ever start conversations with strangers?
▶ Do you think it's odd when a stranger talks to you?
▶ Are you a talkative person?
▶ Do you think you talk too much?
▶ Are you a good listener?
▶ Are you usually the "talker" or the "listener" in a conversation?
▶ What do you like to talk about?
▶ What topics do you try to avoid?

Learning tip *Word webs*

You can use word webs to organize your new vocabulary.

1 Complete the word webs for *clothes* and *food* using words from the box.

✓jacket bread skirt sweatshirt pineapple jeans rice yogurt

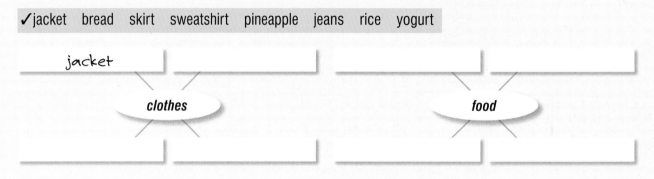

jacket

clothes

food

2 Now make word webs about *colors* and *TV shows*. Write a sentence about each word.

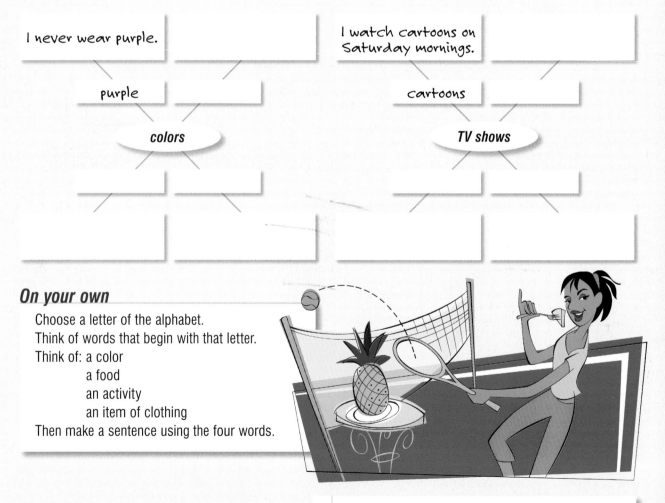

I never wear purple.

purple

colors

I watch cartoons on Saturday mornings.

cartoons

TV shows

On your own

Choose a letter of the alphabet.
Think of words that begin with that letter.
Think of: a color
   a food
   an activity
   an item of clothing
Then make a sentence using the four words.

I play tennis and eat pineapple in pink pants.

Interests

In Unit 2, you learn how to . . .

- use different verb forms.
- use object pronouns, and the pronouns *everybody* and *nobody*.
- talk about your hobbies, interests, and taste in music.
- say *no* in a friendly way.
- use *really* and *not really* to make statements stronger or softer.

Before you begin . . .
Look at the magazine covers. Which magazines would you like to buy? Why?

College News

Meet our new reporter for the *College News*....

The *College News* interviewed Eric Kane, our new reporter. Eric is a full-time student majoring in journalism. We asked him about his hobbies.

❶ *College News:* What are your hobbies?

Eric Kane: Well, I enjoy writing. I like to do a bit of creative writing every day – in the evenings mostly. Someday I want to write a novel, but for now it's just a hobby.

❷ *CN:*

EK: Let's see, what else? Well, I design cards. I'm good at drawing, and I'm really into computer graphics, so I sit and learn new programs, and I play around with them.

❸ *CN:*

EK: Yeah, I play the saxophone, and I can play the piano a little, but not very well. I'd like to play in a jazz band or something. And I like to sing, but I really can't sing at all.

❹ *CN:*

EK: Not really. I prefer to watch sports on TV. I like to play pool. Is that a sport? I guess I jog occasionally. But I hate going to the gym and working out.

❺ *CN:*

EK: Yeah. I love to do new stuff all the time – learn new skills, you know. I'm really excited about writing for the *College News*.

1 Getting started

A Listen to Eric's answers in the interview above. What are the questions? Number the questions, and add them to the interview.

☐ Are you good at sports?   ☐ Are you interested in learning new things?   ☐ Can you play a musical instrument?

☐ What else do you enjoy doing in your free time?   [1] What are your hobbies?

B Listen to the complete interview. What does Eric like to do? What does he hate doing?

Figure it out → **C** Can you complete these sentences with verbs? Which sentences are true for you? Tell a partner.

1. I can _____ the piano.
2. I like _____ sports on TV.
3. I enjoy _____ to music.
4. I'm not good at _____ new computer programs.

2 Grammar Verb forms

Verb	to + verb	Verb + -ing	Preposition + verb + -ing
I can **play** the piano.	I love **to swim**.	I love **swimming**.	I'm good **at drawing** people.
I can't **play** very well.	I like **to play** pool.	I like **playing** pool.	I'm not interested **in skiing**.
I can't **sing** at all.	I hate **to work out**.	I hate **working out**.	
	I prefer **to watch** TV.	I prefer **watching** TV.	
	I'd like **to play** jazz.	I enjoy **reading**.	

A Complete the questions and add two more.

1. Can you ___whistle___ (whistle)?
2. Do you enjoy _____ (cook)?
3. Are you good at _____ (skate)?
4. Do you like _____ (play) board games?
5. Can you _____ (swim)?
6. Are you interested in _____ (join) a meditation class?
7. Do you prefer _____ (exercise) alone or with friends?
8. Would you like _____ (learn) a martial art?
9. _____ ?
10. _____ ?

In conversation . . .

I like / love / hate to + **verb**
is more common than
I like / love / hate + **verb** + *-ing*.

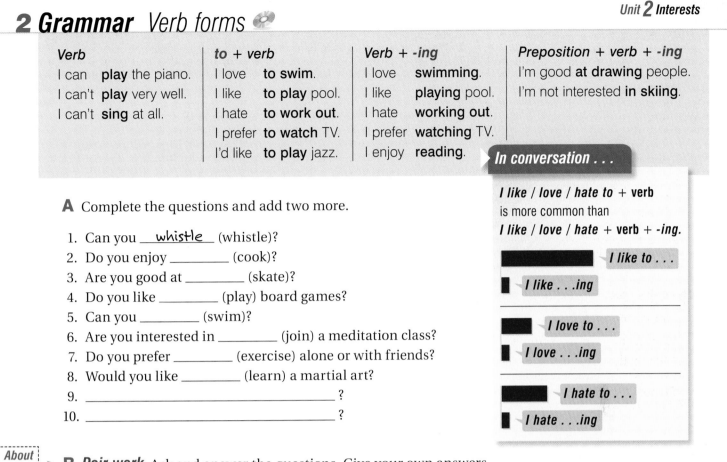

I like to . . .
I like . . .ing

I love to . . .
I love . . .ing

I hate to . . .
I hate . . .ing

About you → **B** *Pair work* Ask and answer the questions. Give your own answers.

A *Can you whistle?*
B *Not very well. What about you? Can you whistle?*

3 Survey

A *Class activity* Ask your classmates about their interests and hobbies. Make notes.

What are your interests?

Find someone who . . .	Name	Notes
is a good dancer.	Marta	likes to dance the tango
likes to read or write poetry.	_____	_____
enjoys driving.	_____	_____
hates doing exercise.	_____	_____
can ride a horse.	_____	_____
is good at learning languages.	_____	_____
would like to learn French.	_____	_____
takes guitar lessons.	_____	_____

"Marta, are you a good dancer?"   *"Yes, I am. I like to dance the tango."*

B Tell the class about someone on your list.

"Marta is a good dancer. She likes to dance the tango."

1 Building vocabulary

A Listen. Number the types of music you hear. What other kinds of music do you know?

| | rock music | **1** | hip-hop and rap | | pop music | | classical music |

| | country music | | folk music | | jazz | | Latin music |

Word sort → **B** Complete the chart with the words above. Add ideas. Then compare with a partner.

I love . . .	I like . . .	I don't care for . . .	I can't stand . . .
rock music			

"I love rock music."   "Yeah, I do too. And I love pop."

2 Speaking naturally *Saying lists*

Jim What kinds of music do you like?

Sam I like classical, and hip-hop, and jazz.   **Sylvia** I like pop, and rock, and folk, . . .

A Listen and repeat the sentences above. Notice that Sam's list is complete, but Sylvia's list is not.

About you → **B** **Class activity** Ask your classmates *What kinds of music do you like?* Take notes. What are the three most popular answers?

3 Building language

A 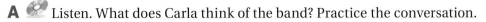 Listen. What does Carla think of the band? Practice the conversation.

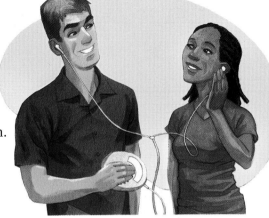

Alex Listen. What do you think of this song?

Carla It's good – I like it. Who is it?

Alex A new band . . . some local guys. Do you like them?

Carla They're local? Really? They're pretty good. Who's the lead singer? I like her. She sounds like Mariah Carey.

Alex Yeah, everybody says that. It's my friend Lori.

Carla Who's the guy singing with her? I'm not sure about him.

Alex Uh . . . actually, that's me. I'm in the band, too.

> **Figure it out**

B Complete the conversations. Then ask a partner your questions. Give your own answers.

1 *A* What do you think of _____ (male singer)?
   B I like _____ .

2 *A* Do you know _____ (female singer)?
   B No, I don't know _____ .

4 Grammar *Object pronouns; everybody, nobody*

I'm a singer. That's **me** on the CD.	It's a nice song. I like **it**.	Everybody ⎤
You're a musician? I'd like to hear **you**.	**We** play in a band. Come listen to **us**.	Everyone ⎟ likes pop.
She's pretty good. I like **her**.	**They**'re local guys. Do you like **them**?	Nobody ⎟
He's not a good singer. I don't like **him**.		No one ⎦

A Complete the questions with object pronouns. Complete the answers with *everybody* or *nobody*. Then practice with a partner.

1. *A* I listen to hip-hop a lot. Do you listen to __it__ , too?
   B Yes. _Everybody_ in my school listens to hip-hop.

2. *A* Ricky Martin – he was on TV last night. Do you know _____ ?
   B Of course I do. _____ knows Ricky Martin.

3. *A* I don't really like classical music. Do you ever listen to _____ ?
   B Yes, but with earphones – _____ in my family likes it.

4. *A* I like Alicia Keys. She's a good singer. What do you think of _____ ?
   B Oh, almost _____ is a fan of Alicia Keys.

5. *A* My favorite band is Coldplay. I think they're great. Do you like _____ ?
   B Yeah. They're the best. _____ plays rock like they do.

> **In conversation . . .**
>
> ***Everybody*** and ***nobody*** are more common than ***everyone*** and ***no one***.
>
> ▬▬▬▬ ⟶ *everybody*
> ▬▬ ⟶ *everyone*
> ─────────
> ▬ ⟶ *nobody*
> ▪ ⟶ *no one*

> **About you**

B *Pair work* Practice again with your own ideas.

"I listen to pop music a lot. Do you listen to it, too?"   *"Yes, I do. I think everybody likes pop music."*

5 Vocabulary notebook *I really like to sing!*

See page 20 for a new way to log and learn vocabulary.

I really like making things.

1 Conversation strategy *Saying no in a friendly way*

A What can you add to this answer to make it sound friendly?

> A **Do you have any hobbies?**
> B **No. _____ .**

🔘 Now listen. What hobbies do Sarah and Matt have?

> Matt **What are you knitting, Sarah?**
>
> Sarah **A sweater. It's for my brother.**
>
> Matt **Nice. Do you make a lot of things?**
>
> Sarah **Yeah. I really enjoy knitting. I guess it's my main hobby. Do you have any hobbies?**
>
> Matt **Um, no. I don't really have much time for hobbies. But I like to take photos. Do you do any photography?**
>
> Sarah **No, not really, um . . . I'm not really into photography. I prefer knitting, sewing, . . . I really like making things. But I'd love to see your pictures sometime.**
>
> Matt **Oh, well, I have some on my computer. Stop by my desk after lunch, and I can show them to you.**

Notice how Sarah and Matt say more than just no when they answer questions. They want to be friendly or polite, so they say more. Find examples in the conversation.

"Um, no. I don't really have much time for hobbies. But I like to . . ."

B Match the questions and answers. Then practice with a partner.

1. Do you have a lot of hobbies? _e_
2. Do you like making things? ____
3. Are you interested in cooking? ____
4. Are you into photography? ____
5. Can you knit or crochet? ____
6. Do you collect anything? ____
7. Are you good at fixing cars? ____

a. Um, no. I'm not really good with my hands.
b. Not really. I'm not very mechanical.
c. No, I don't. A friend of mine collects coins, though.
d. Well, no. I don't even have a camera.
e. No, not really. I don't have a lot of free time.
f. Not really, but I like to bake cakes and things.
g. No, but my sister can. She makes her own sweaters.

About you → **C** *Pair work* Ask and answer the questions. Give your own answers.

"Do you have a lot of hobbies?"   *"Not really, but I enjoy shopping."*

SELF-STUDY
AUDIO CD
CD-ROM

2 Strategy plus *Really*

You can use *really* to make statements stronger and to make negative statements softer.

I really enjoy knitting.

I don't really have much time for hobbies.

Not really can also be a polite way to answer no.

▶ **In conversation . . .**

The top verbs used with *really* are: *enjoy, like, know, think.*

About you → **Pair work** Ask and answer the questions. Give your own answers using *really* or *not really*.

1. Are you interested in sports?
2. Are you into computers?
3. Do you enjoy doing jigsaw puzzles?
4. Are you good at doing crossword puzzles?
5. Can you do anything artistic, like draw or paint?
6. Would you like to learn a new skill, like carpentry?

A *Are you interested in sports?*
B *Well, I really like soccer.* **or** *Not really. I don't really play any sports.*

3 Listening *Different hobbies*

A Do you know anyone with these interests? Would you like to do any of these things? Tell the class.

collecting teddy bears gardening making jewelry playing golf

B Listen to Jeff, Eva, Kim, and Phil. What are their hobbies? Write their names under the pictures.

C Listen again and complete the chart. You can check (✓) more than one name for each question. Then compare with a partner.

	Jeff	Eva	Kim	Phil
1. Who makes money on his / her hobby?	☐	☐	☐	☐
2. Who spends a lot of money on it?	☐	☐	☐	☐
3. Who isn't very good at his / her hobby?	☐	☐	☐	☐
4. Who isn't very enthusiastic about it?	☐	☐	☐	☐

Hobby groups

1 Reading

A Look at the hobby groups on this Web page. Which ones are you interested in?
Tell the class.

Hobby Group Message Board

Hobby Group Message Board   Find a group. [　　　　　] [Search]

(Cars)   (Collecting)   (Cooking)   (Crafts)   (Fashion)   (Music)   (Outdoors)   (Pets)

B Now read these messages. Can you match each message to one of the hobby groups above?

Hobby Group Message Board

From: sushifreak
I want to learn how to make Japanese food.
Do you have any easy recipe ideas?

From: literockfan
I want to get tickets for the Billy Joel concert in Washington. I can pay cash or trade my tickets for the Cher concert in Baltimore in June.

From: handyman
Hi. I make wooden boxes and bowls. I'd like to sell my stuff, but I don't know much about the business side of things. Can you help me?

From: petlover
We have a beautiful gray cat – free to a good home in the New York area. We can't keep her because I just found out I'm allergic to cats.

From: bookworm
I enjoy collecting and reading old books, especially children's books. Please send your old books to me at P.O. Box 614, Salt Springs, Ohio 45640.

From: concernedmom
My son wants to be a race-car driver. Is this safe? Where can I find out more about this?

From: grungeking
I want to find a good place for vintage clothes and jeans. I live in Las Vegas. Any ideas?

From: daredevil
I'd like to try rock climbing, but I don't want to go alone. Is anyone in San Francisco interested in climbing with me? I prefer to go on weekdays, if possible.

C Look at the first line of these replies to the messages. Who are they for? Write the screen names.

Hobby Group Message Board

To: *daredevil*
I'm interested in climbing. I'm not very experienced, but . . .

To:
I have a great Asian recipe book. It's called *Simply Asian*, and . . .

To:
Maybe you can advertise your stuff in a local store, or . . .

To:
There's a great magazine called *Race Track*, and . . .

To:
I have three extra tickets. I prefer to get cash, but . . .

To:
I have a lot of hardbacks and paperbacks. . . .

---

2 *Listening and speaking* Favorite Web sites

A Listen to Joe and Lisa talk about a Web site. What kind of Web site is it? Why does Joe like it?

B Listen again. Choose the correct information to complete the sentences.

1. **25,000 / 55,000** people visit the Web site each day.
2. Joe likes to read the **articles / messages** on the site.
3. Today's article is about hiking in **the U.S. / different countries**.
4. Lisa prefers to **sleep in a tent / stay home**.
5. Joe wants to enter the competition to win a **bike / tent**.

C *Group work* Ask and answer the questions.

- What's your favorite Web site?
- What's interesting about it?
- What other Web sites do you go to a lot?
- Do you ever use Web sites for shopping? banking? doing research?
- Do you have your own Web page or Web site?

3 *Writing* Messages

A Choose a hobby group from the Web page on page 18. Write a question to post on the message board.

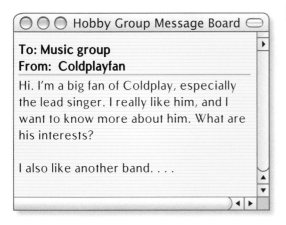

○ ○ ○ Hobby Group Message Board ⊝

To: Music group
From: Coldplayfan

Hi. I'm a big fan of Coldplay, especially the lead singer. I really like him, and I want to know more about him. What are his interests?

I also like another band. . . .

> **Help note**
>
> *Linking ideas*
> - Add an idea:
>   *I listen to music, **and** I like movies.*
>   *I **also** like books, **especially** children's books.*
>   *I don't like jazz **or** rock music.*
> - Contrast two ideas:
>   *I like climbing, **but** my friends don't.*
> - Give a reason:
>   *We can't keep her **because** I'm allergic to*

B Read your classmates' messages. Choose one and reply to it. Then "send" your reply. Do you receive any helpful replies?

4 *Free talk* The game of likes and dislikes

See *Free talk 2* at the back of the book for more speaking practice.

Vocabulary notebook

I really like to sing!

Learning tip *Word chains*

Link new words together in word "chains."

Favorite music

The top 5 types of music people talk about are:
1. rock   4. rap
2. classical   5. country
3. jazz

1 Complete the word chains using the words and expressions below.

playing chess	bake cakes	listen to rock music
skiing	play the guitar	writing poetry

I'm good at → [____] and [____] and [____] .

I don't like to → [____] or [____] or [____] .

2 Now complete the word chains with your own ideas.

I'm good at → [____] and [____] and [____] .

I enjoy → [____] and [____] and [____] .

I can't → [____] or [____] or [____] .

I hate to → [____] and [____] and [____] .

I'd like to → [____] and [____] and [____] .

I'm not interested in → [____] or [____] or [____] .

On your own

Think of different things you are interested in. Can you link them together? Use the last letter of each word or expression to start the next word.

How many words did you use?

sportsoccerocknitting

20

Health

In Unit 3, you learn how to . . .

- use the simple present and present continuous.
- use *if* and *when* in statements and questions.
- talk about health, remedies, sleep habits, and stress.
- encourage people to talk by making comments and asking follow-up questions.
- use expressions like *Wow!* and *You're kidding!* to show surprise.

Before you begin . . .

Which of these things do you do to stay healthy? What else can you do?

- Sleep at least seven hours a night.
- Get a checkup once a year.
- Take regular breaks to cope with stress.
- Eat plenty of fruit and vegetables.

Are you doing anything to stay healthy?

"Well, I generally don't eat a lot of junk food, and I don't eat red meat at all. And right now I'm doing karate. It's getting me in shape quick."

–*Brian Jones*

"Um . . . right now I'm trying to lose weight before my school reunion, so I'm drinking these diet drinks for dinner."

–*Carmen Sanchez*

"Well, I walk everywhere I go because I don't have a car, so I think I get enough exercise."

–*Mei-ling Yu*

"Um . . . to be honest, I'm not doing anything right now. I'm studying for exams this month, so I'm eating a lot of snacks, and I'm not getting any exercise at all."

–*Michael Evans*

"Not really. I kind of eat everything I want. I don't do anything to stay in shape. I'm just lucky, I guess."

–*Lisa da Silva*

"Yeah, we exercise six days a week. We go swimming every other day, and in between we go to the gym. And once in a while, we go hiking."

–*The Parks*

1 Getting started

A 🖸 Listen to these on-the-street interviews. Who do you think has a healthy lifestyle? Why?

Figure it out

B Complete these sentences with a simple present or present continuous verb. Are the sentences true for you? Tell a partner.

1. I usually _____ to the gym twice a week.
2. This month, I _____ a lot of snacks.
3. I generally _____ healthy food.
4. I _____ karate right now.

2 Grammar *Simple present and present continuous*

Use the simple present to talk about "all the time" and routines.	Use the present continuous to talk about "now" and temporary events.
How **do** you **stay** in shape? I **walk** everywhere.	What sports **are** you **playing** these days? I**'m doing** karate. It**'s getting** me in shape.
Do you **get** regular exercise? Yes, I **do**. I **exercise** six days a week. No, we **don't**. We **don't exercise** at all.	**Is** she **trying** to lose weight? Yes, she **is**. She**'s drinking** diet drinks. No, she**'s not**. She**'s not trying** to lose weight.

A Complete the conversations with the simple present or present continuous. Then practice with a partner.

In conversation . . .

The simple present is about 6 times more frequent than the present continuous, and even more frequent with *like*, *love*, *know*, *need*, and *want*.

1 A How _do_ you _cope_ (cope) with stress?

   B Well, I _____ (take) a course in aromatherapy right now, and I _____ (enjoy) it. But everybody in my family is pretty relaxed. We _____ (not get) stressed very often.

2 A What kind of exercise _____ you usually _____ (do)?

   B I _____ (like) swimming. My wife and I usually _____ (go) to the pool every day in the summer. Right now it's cold, so I _____ (not swim) at all. But my wife _____ (go) every day, even when it's cold.

3 A _____ you _____ (eat) a lot of fast food these days?

   B Well, I _____ (love) it, but right now I _____ (try) to eat a balanced diet. It's hard because my husband _____ (not like) fruit and vegetables.

About you → **B** *Pair work* Now ask and answer the questions. Give your own answers.

3 Listening and speaking *Unhealthy habits*

A These people are talking about their unhealthy habits. Try to guess what they're talking about. Then listen and write what they actually say.

1. Ian: "I'm trying to cut down on _____ and _____ ."
2. Kaylie: "I want to give up _____ , but I can't. It's very hard."
3. Martin: "I _____ everywhere. It's bad, I know. I never _____ ."
4. Silvia: "I _____ a lot. I _____ late almost every night."

B Listen again to the last thing each person says. Do you agree? Why or why not? Tell the class.

"I agree with Ian. I think it's good for you." **or** *"I don't agree with Ian because . . ."*

1 Building vocabulary

A Listen and say the sentences. Do you have any of these problems right now?

I have **a fever**. I think I'm getting **the flu**.

I have **a bad cough**. I'm **coughing** a lot.

I have **a stomachache**. I often get stomachaches.

I have **a toothache**.

I hardly ever get **headaches**, but I have one now.

I have **a cold** and **a sore throat**. I get a lot of colds.

I feel **sick**. I often get sick when I eat shellfish.

I have **allergies** and I **sneeze** all the time.

Word sort

B Complete the chart with the words above. Add other ideas. Then compare with a partner.

I never . . .	I hardly ever . . .	I sometimes . . .	I often . . .
get colds			

"I never get colds. Thank goodness!"   *"You're lucky. I often get colds. But I never get the flu."*

2 Speaking naturally Contrasts

A *What's the matter? Do you have a cold?*
B *No, I have a headache. I feel terrible.*
A *That's too bad. I hope you feel better.*
B *Thanks.*

A Listen and repeat the conversation above. Notice how stress shows the contrast between *headache* and *cold*, and between *better* and *terrible*.

B *Pair work* Practice the conversation. Then practice again using different health problems.

3 Building language

A 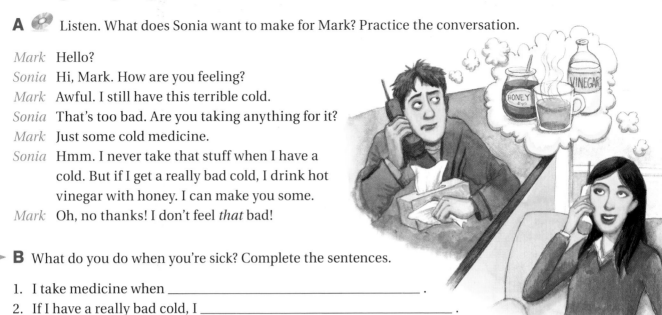 Listen. What does Sonia want to make for Mark? Practice the conversation.

Mark Hello?

Sonia Hi, Mark. How are you feeling?

Mark Awful. I still have this terrible cold.

Sonia That's too bad. Are you taking anything for it?

Mark Just some cold medicine.

Sonia Hmm. I never take that stuff when I have a cold. But if I get a really bad cold, I drink hot vinegar with honey. I can make you some.

Mark Oh, no thanks! I don't feel *that* bad!

Figure it out

B What do you do when you're sick? Complete the sentences.

1. I take medicine when _____ .
2. If I have a really bad cold, I _____ .

4 Grammar *Joining clauses with* if *and* when

What do you take **when** you have a cold?	What do you do **if** you get a really bad cold?
I don't take anything **when** I have a cold.	**If** I get a really bad cold, I drink hot vinegar with honey.
When I have a cold, I don't take anything.	I drink hot vinegar with honey **if** I get a really bad cold.

About you

A Join the phrases with *when* to make true sentences about yourself. Then compare with a partner.

1. have a fever / take medicine
2. get a stomachache / stay in bed
3. have a cough / go to the doctor
4. feel sick / lie down for a while
5. have a sore throat / drink hot tea with honey
6. have a headache / take aspirin

"When I have a fever, I usually take medicine."   *"Really? I never take medicine when I have a fever."*

B Find out what your classmates do in these situations. Use *if* in your questions and answers.

What do they do if they . . .
1. have a bad cold and have to go to class?
2. feel sore after exercising?
3. have a high fever?
4. have an upset stomach after they eat?
5. feel tired and run down?
6. have to cough or sneeze at a concert or movie?

*A **What do you do if you have a bad cold and have to go to class?***
*B **Well, if I have a bad cold, I usually take a lot of tissues to class.***
*C **Really? If I have a bad cold, I just stay home.***

5 Vocabulary notebook *Under the weather*

See page 30 for a new way to log and learn vocabulary.

1 Conversation strategy *Encouraging people to talk*

A Which are the best responses to keep the conversation going? Check (✓) the boxes.

A *I'm so tired.*

B
- [ ] *Yeah, I know.*
- [ ] *Yeah. Me too.*
- [ ] *Really? How come?*

- [ ] *Oh! Why is that?*
- [ ] *Oh, I'm sorry.*
- [ ] *You look tired. Are you busy at work?*

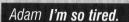 Now listen. Why is Adam tired?

Adam	**I'm so tired.**
Yuki	**Really? How come?**
Adam	**Well, I'm working two jobs this semester, so I'm getting up at, like, 5:30 to study.**
Yuki	**You're kidding! Two jobs? Wow.**
Adam	**Yeah. Just for a couple of months. I'm working in a supermarket after class, and then I have my regular job at the restaurant till 11:00.**
Yuki	**Oh, that's late. So, what time do you go to bed?**
Adam	**About 1:00 . . . 1:30.**
Yuki	**Gosh. So you're only getting about four hours' sleep? That's not much.**

Notice how Yuki encourages Adam to continue talking. She comments on what Adam says and asks follow-up questions. Find examples in the conversation.

"I'm so tired."
"Really? How come?"

B Match each sentence with an appropriate reply. Then practice with a partner.

1. I need a lot of sleep. __d__
2. I can't sleep if there's light in my room. ____
3. I usually go to bed early during the week. ____
4. If I can't fall asleep, I usually read. ____
5. I often take a nap after lunch. ____
6. I only sleep about five hours a night. ____

a. I can't either. Do your windows have blinds?
b. That's not much. Are you getting enough sleep?
c. At the office? How long do you sleep?
d. Really? How much sleep do you need?
e. That's good. Do you wake up early, too?
f. That's a good idea. What do you read?

About you → **C** *Pair work* Student A: Tell a partner about your sleep habits. Use the ideas above. Student B: Respond with comments and questions. Then change roles.

A *I don't really need a lot of sleep.*
B *Really? Me neither. How much sleep do you need?*
A *About five hours a night.*

SELF-STUDY
AUDIO CD
CD-ROM

2 Strategy plus *Showing surprise*

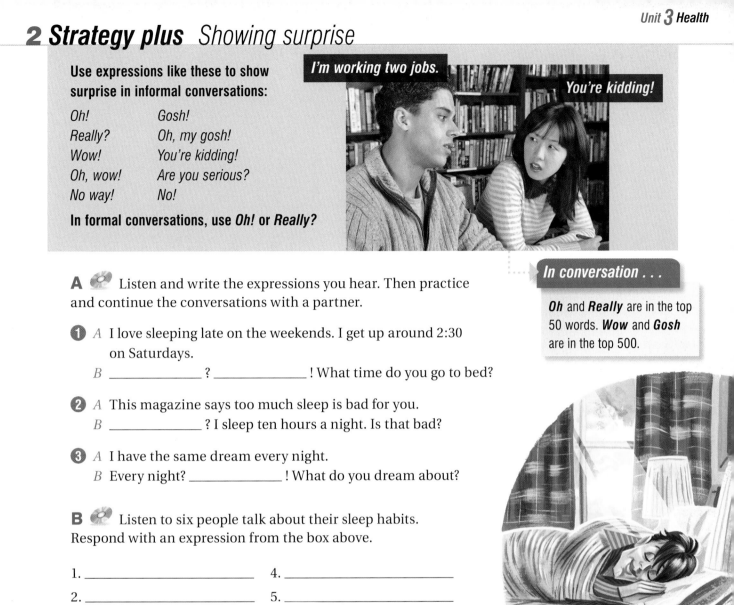

Use expressions like these to show surprise in informal conversations:

Oh!	*Gosh!*
Really?	*Oh, my gosh!*
Wow!	*You're kidding!*
Oh, wow!	*Are you serious?*
No way!	*No!*

In formal conversations, use *Oh!* or *Really?*

I'm working two jobs.

You're kidding!

A Listen and write the expressions you hear. Then practice and continue the conversations with a partner.

In conversation . . .

Oh and *Really* are in the top 50 words. *Wow* and *Gosh* are in the top 500.

1 *A* I love sleeping late on the weekends. I get up around 2:30 on Saturdays.

    B _____ ? _____ ! What time do you go to bed?

2 *A* This magazine says too much sleep is bad for you.

    B _____ ? I sleep ten hours a night. Is that bad?

3 *A* I have the same dream every night.

    B Every night? _____ ! What do you dream about?

B Listen to six people talk about their sleep habits. Respond with an expression from the box above.

1. _____
2. _____
3. _____
4. _____
5. _____
6. _____

3 Talk about it *Sweet dreams?*

Group work Discuss the questions about sleep habits. What do you have in common?

▶ Are you feeling tired today? If so, why?

▶ Do you sleep well, usually?

▶ What do you do if you can't sleep?

▶ Do you ever wake up during the night?

▶ What is your bedtime routine?

▶ Do you ever have vivid dreams or nightmares?

▶ Do you remember your dreams?

▶ Do you snore or talk in your sleep?

▶ Are you a sleepwalker?

4 Free talk *Are you taking care of your health?*

See *Free talk 3* for more speaking practice.

1 Reading

A Do you ever get stressed? How do you feel when that happens? Check (✓) the boxes and add ideas. Then tell the class.

I get stressed when . . .

☐ I'm studying for an exam.   ☐ I have a deadline.
☐ I'm late for an appointment.   ☐ _____ .
☐ I have no money.   ☐ _____ .

When I'm stressed, I . . .

☐ feel tired and irritable.
☐ get a headache.
☐ _____ .

B Read the leaflet. What do you learn about stress? Are any of your ideas mentioned?

COMMON QUESTIONS ABOUT STRESS

Am I stressed?

If you can't sleep well or can't concentrate, . . .

If you feel depressed or want to cry a lot, . . .

If you have a headache or an upset stomach, . . .

If you can't relax and you feel irritable, . . .

If you are extremely tired, . . .

. . . then it's possible you are stressed.

Is stress bad for me?

Occasional stress is common and can be good for you. However, if you feel stressed for a long time, it can be serious. Stress can make you sick. It can also affect your memory or concentration, so work or study is difficult.

What can I do?

Fortunately, there's a lot you can do. Try some of these relaxation techniques. If you still feel stressed, make an appointment to see your doctor.

RELAXATION TECHNIQUES

❶ Breathe Take a breath, hold it for four seconds, and then breathe out very slowly. Feel your body relax.

❷ Exercise Walk or exercise for just 30 minutes each day and feel better.

❸ Talk Call a friend. Talk about your problems.

❹ Meditate Close your eyes and focus on something calm. Feel relaxed.

❺ Pamper yourself Take a hot bath, or have a massage.

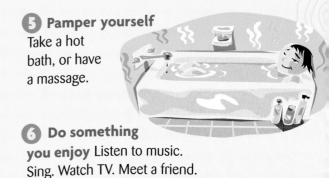

❻ Do something you enjoy Listen to music. Sing. Watch TV. Meet a friend.

Department of Health – "Take care of yourself."

C Read the leaflet again. Answer the questions. Then compare answers with a partner.

1. How can you tell if you are stressed?
2. Why can stress be serious?
3. What can you do if you feel stressed?

4. Which relaxation ideas in the leaflet do you like?
5. Do you think the leaflet is helpful? Why or why not?

2 *Listening* *Time to chill out*

A What do you and your friends do to relax? Do you do any of these things? Tell a partner.

B Listen to four people talk about relaxing. Number the pictures.

C Listen again. What else do they do to relax? Write the activity under each picture.

3 *Writing* *Advice on health*

A Do you have a question about your health? Write a health problem on a piece of paper. Use the ideas below to help you.

I'm feeling stressed about my exams. Help!

I can't sleep at night. What can I do?

I want to get in shape. What can I do?

I get colds all the time. Any suggestions?

B *Group work* Pass your papers around the group. Write a reply to each person.

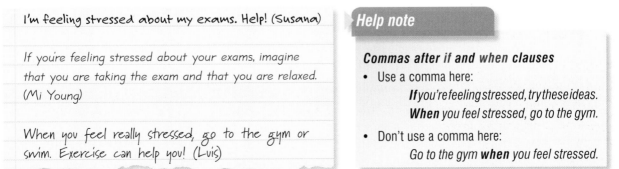

I'm feeling stressed about my exams. Help! (Susana)

If you're feeling stressed about your exams, imagine that you are taking the exam and that you are relaxed. (Mi Young)

When you feel really stressed, go to the gym or swim. Exercise can help you! (Luis)

Help note

Commas after if and when clauses

- Use a comma here:
  If you're feeling stressed, try these ideas.
  When you feel stressed, go to the gym.

- Don't use a comma here:
  Go to the gym **when** you feel stressed.

29

Vocabulary notebook

Under the weather

Learning tip *Learning words together*

When you learn a new word or expression, write down other words you can use with it.

What's the matter?

The top 5 health problems people talk about are:
1. cold   4. flu
2. headache   5. fever
3. allergies

1 Complete these expressions. Use the words in the box.

a break	better	home	in bed	medicine	sick

feel		stay		take	

2 Which of these verbs can you use with the words and expressions in the chart? Complete the chart. You can use some verbs more than once.

be	do	feel	get	go (to)	have	see	stay	take

be feel get	sick		allergies		a vacation
	exercise		a headache		a cough
	a checkup		home		healthy
	stressed		in shape		a doctor

On your own

Go to a drugstore, and look at the medicine. What health problems are they for? Can you remember the names of the health problems in English?

People take this when they have a cough.

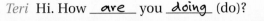

1 Can you complete this conversation?

Complete the conversation. Use the simple present or present continuous. Then practice with a partner.

Teri Hi. How __are__ you __doing__ (do)?

Ruth Not bad. Actually, I _____ (have) a cold again. But I'm OK.

Teri Oh, that's too bad. So, what _____ you _____ (do) today?

Ruth My classmate Sally's here. We _____ (plan) an end-of-term party. Everybody _____ (want) some live music this year. How about you? _____ you _____ (do) anything special today? _____ you _____ (listen) to a CD?

Teri No, that _____ (be) my brother. He _____ (play) his guitar. He _____ (practice) every morning.

Ruth Hey, _____ (be) he free on Saturday? _____ he _____ (want) to play at our party? We _____ (need) somebody like him.

Teri _____ you _____ (kid)? He's only ten!

2 How can you say no?

Add object pronouns to the sentences. Then ask and answer the questions. If your answer is *no*, remember to say *no* in a friendly way.

1. I hate colds, and I get __them__ a lot. Do you get a lot of colds?
2. Some friends and I go to a jazz club every Monday. Do you want to join _____ next week?
3. I have to go to the hospital tomorrow. Can you come with _____ ?
4. My dad wants to paint the house next weekend. Can you help _____ ?
5. I love listening to Norah Jones. She's great! Do you like _____ , too?
6. I'm reading a book about the martial arts. Would you like to borrow _____ sometime?

"Do you get a lot of colds?"   *"Not really. I don't really get sick too often."*

3 How many words do you remember?

A Complete the chart. How many things can you think of for each column?

Types of music you really like	Types of TV shows you often watch	Hobbies you and your friends have	Clothes you don't like to wear	Health problems you sometimes get
rock				

B *Pair work* Take turns discussing the items in your chart. Encourage your partner to talk.

A Well, I really like rock music.

B Really? Who do you listen to? I mean, who are your favorite bands?

31

4 *What do you have in common?*

Complete the sentences with activities. Then compare with a partner. Continue your conversations.

1. I like _____ .
2. I don't enjoy _____ .
3. I'm not good at _____ .
4. I can't _____ .
5. I hate _____ .
6. I'm interested in _____ .

A *I like to play softball. How about you?*
B *Oh, I do too. I play on a team on weekends.*
A *Really? I just play with some friends after work. Actually, we have a game tonight. . . .*

5 *Surprise, surprise!*

Complete the conversation. Use the sentences in the box. Then practice with a partner.

What instruments do you play?	Are you serious?	✓How's school?
Not well, but I'd love to play in a band.	Yeah? I am too.	No way! What kind of music?
Me too. I have my first piano lesson today!	What do you want to do?	

Alice Hi, Carl. How are things?
Carl Great. <u>How's school?</u>
Alice Um, actually, I'm not at school this year.
Carl _____ So, what are you doing?
Alice Well, I'm looking for a job right now.
Carl Really? _____
Alice Well, I'd like to play music in clubs, but –
Carl _____
Alice Well, I play jazz.
Carl No! _____

Alice Saxophone and trumpet. But I really need to find someone to play with me.
Carl I play the piano. _____
Alice You play the piano? That's great. Maybe we can practice together sometime. I'm free this Friday.
Carl _____ What's your phone number?
Alice It's 555-9003. OK, so call me. Oh, look at the time. Sorry, I have to go.
Carl _____

6 *What can you say or do . . . ?*

A *Pair work* What can you say or do in these situations? Do you agree?

What can you say when . . .

- you meet your new neighbors for the first time?
- a new student joins the class and seems nervous?
- the person next to you on the subway looks sick?
- you meet someone interesting at a party?
- you have an umbrella at a bus stop on a rainy day, and the person next to you is getting very wet?

A *What can you say when you meet new neighbors for the first time?*
B *Let me think . . . "Hello." . . . "How are you?" . . . "Would you like some coffee?"*

B *Pair work* Choose a situation. Prepare a short conversation to act out for the class.

Self-check

How sure are you about these areas? Circle the percentages.

grammar
20% 40% 60% 80% 100%
vocabulary
20% 40% 60% 80% 100%
conversation strategies
20% 40% 60% 80% 100%

. . . .

Study plan

What do you want to review? Circle the lessons.

grammar
1A 1B 2A 2B 3A 3B
vocabulary
1A 1B 2A 2B 3A 3B
conversation strategies
1C 2C 3C

Celebrations

In Unit 4, you learn how to . . .

- use *going to* and the present continuous to talk about the future.
- use indirect object pronouns.
- talk about birthdays, celebrations, and favorite holidays.
- use "vague" expressions like *and everything*.
- give "vague" responses like *Maybe* and *It depends*.

Before you begin . . .

Which of these special events are the people celebrating?

- a graduation
- an engagement
- a wedding
- a retirement
- the birth of a baby
- a wedding anniversary

What other special days do people celebrate?

Months ▼		
January	May	September
February	June	October
March	July	November
April	August	December

Days of the month ▼			
1st	first	17th	seventeenth
2nd	second	18th	eighteenth
3rd	third	19th	nineteenth
4th	fourth	20th	twentieth
5th	fifth	21st	twenty-first
6th	sixth	22nd	twenty-second
7th	seventh	23rd	twenty-third
8th	eighth	24th	twenty-fourth
9th	ninth	25th	twenty-fifth
10th	tenth	26th	twenty-sixth
11th	eleventh	27th	twenty-seventh
12th	twelfth	28th	twenty-eighth
13th	thirteenth	29th	twenty-ninth
14th	fourteenth	30th	thirtieth
15th	fifteenth	31st	thirty-first
16th	sixteenth		

Alicia It's Mom's birthday on the first. Remember? She's going to be 50!

Dave Oh, that's right. What are you going to get her?

Alicia I'm going to buy her something special, like a necklace. Then it's Mom and Dad's anniversary on the tenth.

Dave Right. We usually give them something.

Alicia We? You mean, **I** do! Let's, um, send them some flowers.

Dave OK. Then it's my birthday on the twenty-third.

Alicia Yeah, I know. I'm going to get you the same thing you got me – nothing!

1 Getting started

A Listen and say the months and the days of the month. When is your birthday? Circle the month and the day. Tell the class.

"My birthday's in May." **or** *"My birthday's on May tenth."* **or** *"My birthday's on the tenth of May."*

B Listen. What gifts are Alicia and Dave going to buy? Practice the conversation.

Figure it out

C Can you complete the answer to the question? Then practice with a partner.

A What are you going to do for your next birthday?
B I think I'm _____ .

2 Grammar *Future with going to; indirect objects*

I'm **going to** buy something special.
You're **going to** get a present.
She's **going to** be 50.
We're **going to** send some flowers.
They're **going to** have a party.

What **are** you **going to** do for your birthday?
I'm **not going to** do anything special.
Are you **going to** have a party?
Yes, we **are**. We're **going to** invite all our friends.
No, we're **not**. We're **not going to** do much.

Indirect objects

I'm going to buy **my mother** something special.
Alicia isn't going to give **Dave** anything.
Let's send **Mom and Dad** some flowers.

Indirect object pronouns:
me, you, him, her, us, them

I'm going to buy **her** something special.
Alicia isn't going to give **him** anything.
Let's send **them** some flowers.

About you → **A** Complete the questions using *going to*. Then write your own answers, using indirect object pronouns where necessary.

1. _____ you _____ do anything special for your next birthday?
2. _____ you _____ invite your friends over for a party?
3. _____ someone _____ bake you a birthday cake?
4. _____ your parents _____ buy you something nice?
5. How old _____ your parents _____ be on their next birthdays?
6. What _____ you _____ give your father for his birthday?
   How about your mother? And your best friend?

B *Pair work* Ask and answer the questions.

A **Are you going to do anything special for your next birthday?**
B *Yeah. My friends are going to buy me dinner at a Thai restaurant.*

3 Speaking naturally *going to*

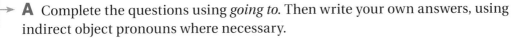

What are you going to do tonight?   Are you going to go to the movies?   I'm going to stay home.

A Listen and repeat the sentences above. Notice the ways of saying *going to*.

About you → **B** Listen. Match the two parts of each question. Then ask a partner the questions.

1. Are you going to _ e _
2. How many cards are you going to ____
3. Are you going to ____
4. Who are you going to ____
5. Are you going to ____

a. spend your next birthday with?
b. send anyone flowers this year?
c. send this year?
d. send anyone a card this month?
e. buy anyone a gift this month?

A **Are you going to buy anyone a gift this month?**
B *Yeah, my brother. His birthday is on the fifth. I think I'm going to buy him a watch.*

1 Building vocabulary

Word sort ▸

A What do people do on these special days? Find two expressions from the box for each event. What else do people do? Add ideas.

blow out candles on a cake	go out for a romantic dinner	shout "Happy New Year"
give someone chocolates	go to see fireworks	sing "Happy Birthday"
exchange rings	go trick-or-treating	wear a cap and gown
get a degree or diploma	have a reception	✓ wear a costume

❶

Halloween

wear a costume
_____
_____

❷

Valentine's Day

_____
_____
_____

❸

birthday

_____
_____
_____

❹

graduation day

_____
_____
_____

❺

New Year's Eve

_____
_____
_____

❻

wedding day

_____
_____
_____

About you ▸

B *Pair work* Talk about special days or events you are going to celebrate this year. When are they? How are you going to celebrate them?

A I'm going to have a Halloween party in October.
B Is everybody going to wear costumes? **or** *Are you going to go trick-or-treating, too?*

2 Building language

A  Listen to Marcella's phone message. What are her plans for New Year's Eve?

Voice mail Hi. This is Laurie. Please leave a message after the beep. Thanks for calling.

Marcella Hi, Laurie. This is Marcella. Listen, what are you doing tomorrow night? A group of us are going out for dinner and then to a big New Year's Eve party. Do you want to come? We're meeting at the restaurant at 8:30, and we're probably going to go to the party around 11:00. It's going to be a lot of fun. So call me back, OK? Oh, and by the way, they say it's going to snow tomorrow, so be careful. Bye.

Figure it out

B Find Marcella's plans. Find the weather prediction. What verb forms does she use?

3 Grammar *Present continuous for the future; going to*

> **You can use the present continuous or going to to talk about plans.**
> **The present continuous is often used for plans with specific times or places.**
>
> What **are** you **doing** for New Year's Eve?   What **are** you **going to do** for New Year's Eve?
>   We**'re going to** The Sea Grill for dinner.   We**'re going to go** somewhere for dinner.
>   We**'re meeting** friends there at 8:30.   We**'re going to meet** some friends at a restaurant.
>
> **You can also use going to for predictions.**
>
> It's **going to** be fun. (NOT It's being fun.)   It's **going to** snow tomorrow. (NOT It's snowing tomorrow.)

A Match each plan with a prediction. Then role-play with a partner. Ask follow-up questions.

1. My best friend's getting married in May. __c__
2. We're going trick-or-treating on Halloween. _____
3. My parents are going to get me something special for graduation. _____
4. My sister's graduating from law school soon. _____
5. I'm going to get my dad a tie for his birthday. _____

a. I think he's going to love it!
b. She's going to be a great lawyer.
c. It's going to be a fun wedding.
d. It's going to rain, but we don't care.
e. I think they're going to get me a laptop.

A *My best friend's getting married in May. It's going to be a fun wedding.*
B *Oh. Where are they having the reception?*

About you

B *Pair work* Find out about each other's plans for next weekend and the next holiday.

"What are you doing on Friday night?"   *"I'm meeting a friend. We're going to go to a club."*

4 Vocabulary notebook *Calendars*

See page 42 for a new way to log and learn vocabulary.

1 *Conversation strategy* "Vague" expressions

A What do you think the underlined expression means? Check (✓) two ideas.

We have a lot of festivals <u>and things like that</u>.

☐ hobbies ☐ celebrations ☐ holidays

Now listen. What happens during the fiesta?

Ray **Are you going to the fiesta this weekend?**

Tina **I don't know. It depends. What is it exactly?**

Ray **Well, it's just, um . . . it's a festival. It's lots of parades and stuff like that. Everybody gets dressed up, you know. . . .**

Tina **You mean in costumes?**

Ray **Yeah. There are hundreds of cute little kids in purple and silver outfits with makeup and everything. . . .**

Tina **Uh-huh. Uh, I'm not big on parades.**

Ray **And there's good food. You can get all kinds of tacos and things. Do you want to go?**

Tina **Hmm. Well, maybe.**

Notice how Ray uses "vague" expressions like *and everything* and *and things (like that)*. He doesn't need to give Tina a complete list. Find examples in the conversation.

"You can get all kinds of tacos and things."

B What do the "vague" expressions mean in these conversations? Choose two ideas from the box for each one. Then practice with a partner.

> **In conversation . . .**
>
> People often say **and stuff** in very informal situations.
> **and stuff** ■ ■ ■ ■ ■ ■ ■   **and things** ■ ■ ■

| anniversaries | concerts | dancing | ✓ holidays | sing "Happy Birthday" |
| candles | cultural events | folk songs | see old friends | spend time at home |

❶ *A* Do you go to a restaurant to celebrate birthdays *and stuff*? holidays
   B Yeah, we know a nice place. They bring out cakes *and everything*.

❷ *A* Are you into traditional music *and stuff like that*?
   B Yeah, we have a lot of music festivals *and things like that* around here.

❸ *A* What are you doing for New Year's?
   B I'm going home. I really want to see my family *and everything*.

SELF-STUDY
AUDIO CD
CD-ROM

2 Strategy plus *"Vague" responses*

You can use responses like these if you're not sure about your answer:
I don't know.
I'm not sure.
Maybe.
It depends.

Are you going to the fiesta this weekend?

I don't know. It depends. What is it exactly?

▶ *In conversation . . .*

I don't know and *I'm not sure* are more common responses than *Maybe* and *It depends*.

███████████	▸ **I don't know.**
██████████	▸ **I'm not sure.**
███████	▸ **Maybe.**
██	**It depends.**

Group work Choose a festival or holiday. Discuss the questions. Use "vague" responses if you need to.

- When is it?
- What does it celebrate?
- How do people celebrate?
- Do they eat any special foods?
- Do they wear costumes or put up decorations?
- How are you going to celebrate it next time?

A **What about Mardi Gras? Let's talk about that.**
B **OK. So, when is it?**
C **It depends. It's different every year.**

3 Listening *Celebrations around the world*

Look at the pictures of these two festivals. What's happening? Then listen and answer the questions.

	1 Santa Lucia Day	**2** Bonfire Night
What country is it in?	It's in Sweden.	
When is it?		
What do people do?		

4 Free talk *A new celebration*

See *Free talk 4* for more speaking practice.

1 Reading

A Brainstorm! How many words can you think of related to these celebrations? Make a class list.

weddings   **birthdays**   **New Year's Eve**

weddings: bride, groom, flower girl

B Read the article. Which of your words can you find?

Time to celebrate!

New Year

Children in **Taiwan** love Chinese New Year because they know they are going to get *hong bao* from their relatives. *Hong bao* are red envelopes with money inside.

In **Ecuador**, people say good-bye to the old year by burning life-size dummies dressed in old clothes on big bonfires. Young people dress up as widows, witches, or skeletons and ask for money for fireworks for the New Year's celebrations.

Weddings

In **Colombia**, the bride and groom each light a candle. Then they light a third candle together and blow out the first two. This third candle means that they are now one and are going to share their lives together.

Birthdays

In **Korea** on a baby's first birthday, parents put things like money, thread, and pencils in front of their baby. If the baby picks up the money, it means he or she is going to be rich. Choosing the thread means a long life for the baby, and choosing a pencil means he or she is going to be a good student.

In the **United Kingdom**, **Australia**, and **North America**, brides wear "something old, something new, something borrowed, and something blue" for good luck.

In **Turkey**, the female friends of the bride write their names inside her shoes. After the wedding ceremony, the bride looks inside her shoes. If she can no longer read one of her friends' names, it means that friend is going to get married next.

C Read the article again. Can you find these things? Compare answers with a partner.

1. three traditions about money
2. three traditions about clothes
3. three traditions using fire
4. the words for two people who get married

About you → **D** *Group work* Discuss the questions about traditions.

- What traditions do you have for weddings? What do brides wear?
- Which birthdays are special? How do people celebrate them?
- What traditions do you have for New Year's? What brings good luck?

2 *Listening and writing* Congratulations!

A Listen to the people open their invitations to these events. Complete the information.

❶

You're invited to
a housewarming party!

for __Elaine Collins__

on _____

at _____ **p.m.** _____

at __1452 E. Mulberry St.__

Hi Simon and Julie,
I'm finally ready to entertain! I'm having
a barbecue. Sally is going to bring some
_____ . Simon, can you make some
of your special _____ ?
Thanks!
See you then,
Elaine

❷

In celebration of their
_____ *wedding anniversary,*
Iris and Derek
invite you to dinner

on _____

at _____ p.m.

at The _____ Restaurant.

R.S.V.P.

Dear John and Jessie,
Hope you can make it to the dinner. There's going
to be _____ and _____ afterwards.
We're looking forward to seeing you both.
Regards,
Iris and Derek

B Invite a friend to a special event. Write an invitation like the ones above, and add a personal note.

> **Help note**

Writing personal notes		
	Less formal	**More formal**
Start like this:	**Dear** *(name),*	**Dear** *(name),*
	Hi *(name),*	
End like this:	**Take care,**	**Best wishes,**
	See you,	**Best regards,**
	Love,	**All the best,**

C *Group work* Exchange invitations. Which invitation is the most popular in your group? Tell the class.

Vocabulary notebook

Calendars

Learning tip *Linking events with dates*

You can write down some of your new vocabulary on a calendar. It's a useful way to learn the names of special events and celebrations.

1 Complete the calendar with words from the box.

card	vacation	Eve	February	fireworks	November	graduation	anniversary
May	dinner	✓ flowers	September	Halloween	retirement	Valentine's	gown

January
11th – *Mom's birthday. Buy her* __flowers__ *and a cake.*

_____ 14th – _____ *Day!*

March
23rd – *Suzanne's birthday. Go out for* _____ .

April
1st – *April Fools' Day*

_____ 4th – *My birthday!*

June
2nd – *End of exams*
21st – *School* _____ .
Rent a cap and _____ .

July
1st – *Summer* _____ *starts.*
22nd – *Dad's 65th birthday and* _____ *party*

August
16th – *Summer party and* _____ *at night*

_____ 10th – *Jack and Betty's wedding* _____ . *Send them a* _____ .

October
31st – _____

_____ 29th – *Family reunion for Thanksgiving*

December
31st – *New Year's* _____ *party*

2 Now make your own calendar. Note important dates and plans in your year.

On your own

Buy a wall calendar. Circle your important dates, and write the things you are going to do in English. Put it on the wall so you can see it.

Growing up

In Unit 5, you learn how to . . .

- use the simple past in statements and questions (review).
- use time expressions to talk about the past.
- use *all*, *most*, *a lot of*, *a few*, etc.
- talk about memories of childhood, school, and your teenage years.
- correct yourself with expressions like *Wait*, *Actually*, and *I mean*.

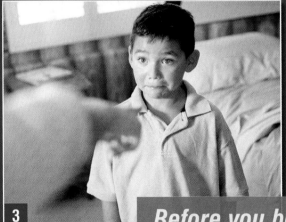

Before you begin . . .

Do you have memories like these? Do you remember . . .

- sleepovers with your friends?
- learning to swim?
- a time you got into trouble?
- your first close friend?

Ramon That's a great baseball shirt, Ling.
Are you from Seattle?

Ling Um, kind of. I lived there, but
I wasn't born there.

Ramon Oh, yeah? Where were you born?

Ling In São Paulo, actually.

Ramon São Paulo? Brazil?

Ling Yeah. My parents were born in
Hong Kong, but they moved to
São Paulo in 1986, just before
I was born.

Ramon Wow. How long did you live there?

Ling Until I was six. Then we moved to
the U.S.

Ramon To Seattle?

Ling Yeah. We lived there for ten
years, and we came here to San
Francisco about three years ago.

Ramon Huh. So did you grow up bilingual?

Ling Well, we always spoke Chinese
at home. I couldn't speak English
until I went to school. And actually,
I can still speak a little Portuguese.

1 Getting started

A  Listen. Where was Ling born? Where does she live now? Practice the conversation.

Figure it out → **B** Can you complete the sentences? Use the conversation above to help you.

1. Ling's family left Hong Kong _____ 1986.
2. Ling lived in São Paulo _____ six years.
3. Her family stayed there _____ she was six.
4. They moved to Seattle. _____ they came to San Francisco.
5. They moved to San Francisco three years _____ .

2 Grammar *be born; simple past (review); time expressions*

Where **were** you **born**?
   I **was born** in São Paulo.
   I **wasn't born** in Seattle.

Where **were** your parents **born**?
   They **were born** in Hong Kong.
   They **weren't born** in the U.S.

Did you live there **for a long time**?
   Yes, (I did). I lived there **for six years**.
   No, (I didn't). I didn't live there **long**.

How long did you live in São Paulo?
   We lived there **until** I was six. **From** 1986 **to** 1992.
   We didn't leave **until** 1992. **Then** we came to the U.S.

Did she move here **last year**?
   Yes, (she did). She moved **in May**.
   No, (she didn't). She moved **in 2002**.

When did they come here?
   They came here about **three years ago**.
   They came **when** Ling was sixteen.

A Complete the sentences with time expressions so they are true for you. Then compare with a partner.

> **Saying years**
>
> 1906 = "Nineteen oh-six"
> 1988 = "Nineteen eighty-eight"
> 2007 = "Two thousand (and) seven"
> 2015 = "Twenty fifteen"

1. I learned to ride a bicycle in __1988__ , when __I was seven__ .
2. My best friend was born _____ ago, in _____ .
3. I played a musical instrument for _____ ,
   until _____ .
4. I went to elementary school until _____ ,
   from _____ to _____ .
5. My family last went on vacation together in _____ , when _____ .

B Complete the questions. Then ask and answer the questions with a partner.

1. Where _____ your mother born?
   _____ your father born there, too?

2. Where _____ you grow up?
   _____ you born there?

3. Who _____ your best friend in school?
   How long _____ you best friends?

4. _____ you and your best friend ever fight?
   _____ you ever get in trouble?

5. Who took care of you when you _____ little?
   _____ your mother have a job?

3 Speaking naturally *did you*

Where *did you* go on vacation?   What *did you* do?   *Did you* have fun?

A Listen and repeat the questions above. Notice the ways of saying *did you*.

B Listen and complete the questions about your childhood vacations. Then ask and answer the questions with a partner.

When you were a child, . . .
1. Did you _____ ?
2. Where did you _____ ?
3. Who did you _____ ?
4. How long did you _____ ?
5. Did you _____ ?
6. What did you _____ ?

Favorite classes

1 Building language

A 🎧 Listen. What languages did these people study in school?

What languages did you learn in school?

Keiko

All the students in my high school had to take English – it was required. And I needed English to get into my university. (Tokyo)

Mirka

Well, years ago, most people learned Russian and only a few people took English. I studied both. (Warsaw)

Brad

I took Spanish last year, and most of my friends did, too. There are a lot of Spanish speakers around here, so it's kind of useful. (Los Angeles)

Paul

A lot of my classmates dropped French after ninth grade. Almost all of them – except me. But then later, some of them had to take evening classes because they needed it for work. (Lagos)

Figure it out

B Circle the correct expression to complete these sentences. Are they true for you?

1. **Most / Most of** my friends are fluent in English.   2. **A few / A few of** people in my city know Russian.

2 Grammar Determiners 🎧

General		Specific			
All	**children** learn a language.	**All (of)**	**the children in my town** take English.	**All of**	**them** . . .
Most	**Canadians** need French.	**Most of**	**the people in my office** know French.	**Most of**	**us** . . .
Some	**students** take Spanish.	**Some of**	**the students in my class** take Greek.	**Some of**	**us** . . .
A few	**people** are good at Latin.	**A few of**	**my classmates** got As.	**A few of**	**them** . . .
No	**students** like exams.	**None of**	**my friends** failed the exams.	**None of**	**them** . . .
But:					
A lot of	**people** speak English well.	**A lot of**	**the people in this city** speak English.	**A lot of**	**them** . . .

About you

Make true sentences using determiners. Compare with a partner.

1. _____ my friends studied English in junior high school.
   _____ junior high school students take English.
2. Today _____ employees need a second language for their jobs.
   _____ my friends speak two languages.
3. _____ college students major in languages.
   _____ the colleges here teach several different languages.
4. _____ students take two languages in high school.
   In my class, _____ us studied two languages.

In conversation . . .

People usually say **everybody** and **nobody**, not **all people** or **no people**.

3 *Building vocabulary*

A 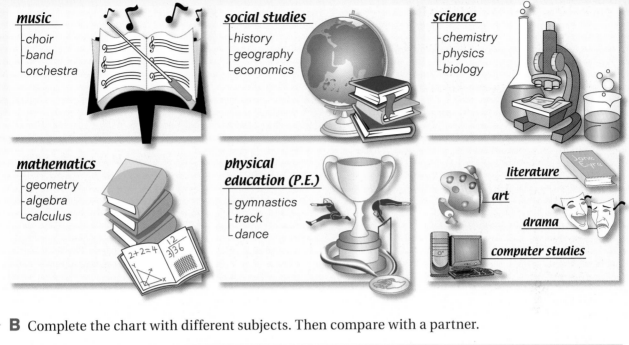 Listen and say the subjects. Can you think of other subjects and categories? Which subjects are you interested in? Tell the class.

music
- choir
- band
- orchestra

social studies
- history
- geography
- economics

science
- chemistry
- physics
- biology

mathematics
- geometry
- algebra
- calculus

physical education (P.E.)
- gymnastics
- track
- dance

literature

art

drama

computer studies

Word
sort

B Complete the chart with different subjects. Then compare with a partner.

I like / liked . . .	I don't like / didn't like . . .	I'd like to study . . .
algebra	geography	

4 *Survey* *What were your best subjects?*

A Class activity Complete the questions with different subjects. Then ask your classmates the questions. Keep a tally of the answers. If you are still in high school, talk about last year.

	Yes	No
Did you study __chemistry__ ?	⊪⊩	‖
Were you good at _____ ?		
Did you get good grades in _____ ?		

	Yes	No
Were your _____ classes hard ?		
Did you enjoy _____ ?		
Did you hate _____ ?		

B Tell the class your results. What interesting information do you learn?

"Most of us studied chemistry. Only a few people were good at physics. . . ."

5 *Vocabulary notebook* *I hated math!*

See page 52 for a new way to log and learn vocabulary.

1 Conversation strategy   *Correcting things you say*

A Can you think of possible ways to complete these replies?

A   *How old were you when you moved here?*
B   *I was seven. Actually, no, I was _____ .*

A   *Who took you to school on your first day?*
B   *My mom. No, wait, my _____ took me.*

Now listen. What does Ben remember about his first day of school?

Ben   **Look at these old photos. My mom sent them to me.**

Jessica   *Oh, is this you?*

Ben   **Yeah, with my best friend. We were in kindergarten together.**

Jessica   *Oh, . . . you were cute! Do you remember much about kindergarten?*

Ben   **Not really. Well, I remember my first day of school. Actually, I don't remember the day, but I remember on the way home I missed my bus stop.**

Jessica   *Oh, no!*

Ben   **Yeah. And I kept riding around until I was the last kid on the bus.**

Jessica   *So how did you get home?*

Ben   **Well, the teacher, I mean, the bus driver, had to call and find out my address and everything, and he took me home.**

Jessica   *So that was when you were five?*

Ben   **Yeah. Uh . . . no, wait. . . . I was only four. I started school early.**

Notice how Ben corrects the things he says with expressions like these: *Well*; *Actually*; *No, wait*. Find examples in the conversation.

> "No, wait. . . . I was only four."

B Match the sentences with the corrections. Then compare with a partner.

1. I don't remember anything about my childhood.   _e_
2. I started gymnastics when I was five. _____
3. I hated swimming lessons. _____
4. I lived with my grandparents for a year. _____
5. I played piano until I was ten. _____
6. All my friends were very nice. _____

a. Actually, no, I was 11 when I quit.
b. Well, they were OK, but I was always scared
c. Well, most of them, not all of them.
d. No, wait. I was six.
e. Well, actually, I remember a few things.
f. No, wait. Actually, it was two years.

About you   **C Pair work** Tell a partner three things about your childhood, but make a few mistakes. Correct the information with *Well*; *Actually*; or *No, wait*.

SELF-STUDY
AUDIO CD
CD-ROM

2 Strategy plus *I mean*

You can use *I mean* to correct yourself when you say the wrong word or name. This is just one use of *I mean*.

> Well, the teacher, I mean, the bus driver, had to . . .

In conversation . . .

Mean is one of the top 100 words. About 90% of its uses are in the expression *I mean*.

A Complete the questions by correcting the underlined words. Use the words on the right.

When you were a child, . . .

1. Did you read a lot of <u>cartoons</u>, I mean, <u>comic books</u> ?
2. Did you have a <u>motorbike</u>, I mean, a _____ ?
3. How often did you visit your <u>parents</u>, I mean, your _____ ?
4. Did you go <u>skiing</u> in the winter, I mean, _____ ?
5. Were you afraid of <u>cats</u>, I mean, _____ ?
6. Did you have an imaginary <u>classmate</u>, I mean, _____ ?
7. Did you collect <u>animals</u>, I mean, _____ ?
8. Were you good at playing <u>chess</u>, I mean, _____ ?

stuffed animals
checkers
friend
mountain bike
skating
✓ comic books
dogs
grandparents

About you

B *Pair work* Ask and answer the questions. Continue your conversations.

"Did you read a lot of cartoons, I mean, comic books?"   *"Yes, I did. My favorite was . . ."*

3 Listening and speaking *I don't remember exactly . . .*

A Listen to people talk about their childhood memories. Underline the words they correct. Write the corrections on the lines.

1. When I was <u>three</u>, we moved to another city for a few years. <u>four</u>
2. I played softball until I was in sixth grade, and then I got interested in other sports, like football. _____
3. My mother made clothes for me and my brother. One time, she made me some dark blue shorts. They were awful. _____
4. I met my best friend in 1996. We were in high school together. _____
5. All the kids teased me in school because I had an unusual name. But one kid was really nice to me. _____

About you

B *Pair work* Take turns telling memories of growing up. Ask questions to find out more information.

"I got into trouble one time."   *"Oh? What did you do?"*

4 Free talk *In the past*

See *Free talk 5* for more speaking practice.

Teenage years

1 Reading

A Brainstorm the word *teenager*! What do you think of? Make a class list.

teenager: parties, loud music, fights with parents

B Read the interview. Which of Jennifer's answers are funny? Which are interesting?

AN **INTERVIEW** WITH . . .
Jennifer Wilkin

Jennifer works in publishing. We asked her about her memories of being a teenager.

Did you enjoy being a teenager?
It was mostly OK, but I had some difficulties, like everyone else. When you're a teenager, you're unsure of yourself.

What were the fashions then?
I was a teenager in the '80s, and so the clothes were very colorful. I was a fashion rebel, though – I always wore black, and I wore a lot of cheap silver jewelry. Often I wore vintage clothing.

What kind of music did you listen to?
My tastes were varied – I was a classical violinist, but I listened to punk rock and new wave music. I had all my "weird" cassette tapes, and I was never without them.

What's your best memory from your teenage years?
I guess it was a trip I took every summer with my youth group. It was a time to travel, be with close friends, and be away from my parents.

And your worst?
I think going to school was the worst. I'm not a social type, and it gave me all kinds of anxiety.

What's one thing you remember about school?
I remember that everybody tried to be different, but they tried to be the same, also.

What was your favorite subject?
My favorite subject was psychology. I loved analyzing my friends.

Were you ever in trouble? Why?
I got detention lots of times because I was late for school every morning, but I never got in real trouble.

How did you spend your free time?
Actually, I spent a lot of time driving around in friends' cars, honking at people's houses as we drove by. I also spent time reading, playing with my dog and cat, or tormenting my younger sister.

What do you miss about your teenage days?
NOTHING! Except my jeans size.

What's one piece of advice you would give to today's teenagers?
Get off your computer, and turn off the TV!

C Add these missing sentences to the interview with Jennifer. Write the numbers in the spaces.

❶ I have no idea now why we did that!

❷ I was always happy to get home, though.

❸ I tried my best to look different.

❹ I hardly ever listened to the radio.

❺ And you're always trying to fit in.

2 *Listening* A long time ago

Listen to Colin talk about being a teenager in England many years ago. Complete the sentences by circling *a*, *b*, or *c*.

1. Colin was a teenager	a. in the '40s.	b. in the '50s.	c. in the '60s.
2. He quit school when he was	a. 13.	b. 14.	c. 15.
3. His first job was	a. in a factory.	b. in a store.	c. on a farm.
4. His main interest was	a. music.	b. buying clothes.	c. watching TV.
5. His main regret is that he	a. spent a lot of money.	b. didn't take classes.	c. didn't have fun.

3 *Writing* An interview

A Write five interview questions to ask a classmate about when he or she was younger. Leave spaces for the answers.

> 1. Did you get along with your parents?
>
> 2. Were you a good student?

B Exchange your questions with a classmate. Write answers to your classmate's questions.

> 1. Did you get along with your parents?
> Yes, I did. I was busy, so I didn't see them much. We agreed on most things except for the car. We had a lot of fights about that.

Help note

Linking ideas: *except (for), apart from*

*We agreed on most things **except for** the car.*

*We didn't agree on much **apart from** my best friend. They liked her.*

C *Pair work* Now read your partner's answers. Ask questions to find out more information.

Vocabulary notebook

Learning tip *Grouping vocabulary*

You can group new vocabulary in different ways to help you remember it. For example, group things you can or can't do, or things you are interested in or not interested in.

The top 4 school subjects people talk about are:
1. math   3. physics
2. science   4. history
People say **math** almost 10 times more than **mathematics**.

1 Complete the chart with these school subjects.

biology	chemistry	English	geography	history
math	physics	P.E.	art	music

I'm / I was good at . . .	*I'm not / I wasn't very good at . . .*	*I can't / I couldn't do . . . at all.*

2 Now complete this chart. Use the school subjects above, and add more.

I like / liked . . .	*I hate / hated . . .*	*I'm not / I wasn't really interested in . . .*

On your own

Walk around a large bookstore, and look at the different sections. How many subjects do you know in English?

52

Around town

In Unit 6, you learn how to . . .

- use *Is there?* and *Are there?* to ask about places in a town.
- use location expressions like *across from* and *outside*.
- use *Can* and *Could* to offer help and ask for directions.
- talk about stores and favorite places in your city or town.
- check information by repeating key words, using "checking" expressions and asking "echo" questions.

Before you begin . . .

Match each comment with a picture.

| | "There's a lot to see." | | "It's great for shopping." |
| "It's easy to get around." | | "There's a lot of nightlife." |

What else can you say about each place?

Out shopping

THIRD AVENUE

Happy Planet Internet Café

Xtreme Video F U Arcade

Riviera Shoes

Richman's Jewelry

Full Moon Karaoke Club

Freeman's Department Store

MAIN STREET

Drugstore

All-Rex

LINCOLN STREET

SECOND AVENUE

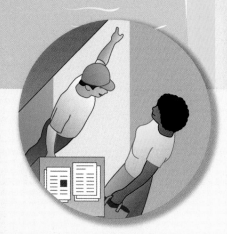

Woman Excuse me, please. Is there an Internet café near here?

Jack Uh . . . there's one on Main Street – across from the big department store. It's right up this street.

Woman Thanks. Oh, and are there any cash machines around here?

Jack Yeah. There are some ATMs over there outside the bank, just across the street.

Woman Oh, yeah. I see them. Thanks.

BEACH STREET

Lucky Stars Sports Café

Beach Cinema

Dino's Supermarket

Eddie's Electronics

Lee's Flower Shop

Sasso Gas

parking $5.00 an hour

Pacific Bank

ATM

Sam's Deli

& Convenience Store

FIRST AVENUE

1 Getting started

A How often do you go to places like the ones above? What can you do or buy in these places? Tell the class.

B 🖸 Listen. A woman is asking Jack for help. What is she looking for? Practice the conversation.

Figure it out ➞ **C** Can you complete these questions and answers? Practice with a partner.

❶ *Boy* __Is there__ a video arcade near here?

Jack Yes, there's _____ on Beach Street.

❷ *Man* _____ any pay phones around here?

Jack Yes, there are _____ in front of the Happy Planet Internet Café.

54

2 *Grammar* Is there? Are there?; *location expressions*

Is there an Internet café near here? Yes, there is. There's **one** on Main Street. It's across from the department store. No, there isn't **(one)**.	**Are there any** cash machines near here? Yes, there are. There are **some** outside the bank. Yes, there's **one** over there. No, there aren't **(any)**.

A Look at the map on page 54. Complete the questions with *Is there a* or *Are there any*. Complete the answers with *one, some, any,* and location expressions. Then practice with a partner.

> **Location expressions**

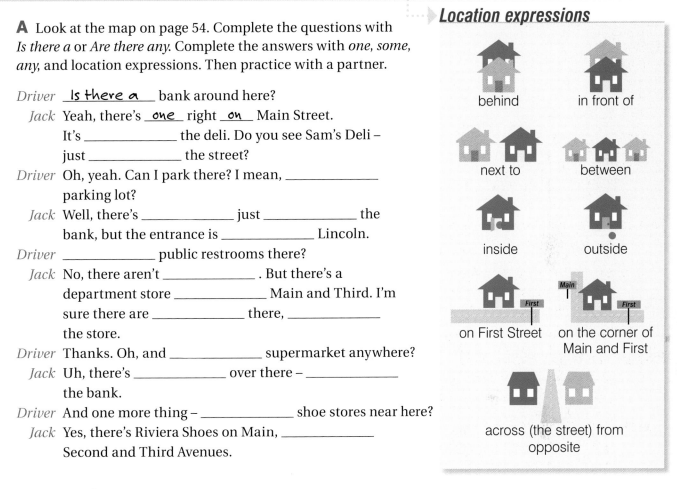

Driver <u>Is there a</u> bank around here?

Jack Yeah, there's <u>one</u> right <u>on</u> Main Street.
It's _____ the deli. Do you see Sam's Deli –
just _____ the street?

Driver Oh, yeah. Can I park there? I mean, _____
parking lot?

Jack Well, there's _____ just _____ the
bank, but the entrance is _____ Lincoln.

Driver _____ public restrooms there?

Jack No, there aren't _____ . But there's a
department store _____ Main and Third. I'm
sure there are _____ there, _____
the store.

Driver Thanks. Oh, and _____ supermarket anywhere?

Jack Uh, there's _____ over there – _____
the bank.

Driver And one more thing – _____ shoe stores near here?

Jack Yes, there's Riviera Shoes on Main, _____
Second and Third Avenues.

Location expressions labels: behind, in front of, next to, between, inside, outside, on First Street, on the corner of Main and First, across (the street) from, opposite

B *Pair work* Now ask and answer questions about these places on the map.

a jewelry store   restaurants   a karaoke club   gas stations   an electronics store

3 *Speaking naturally* Word stress in compound nouns

bookstore   **rest**room   **pay** phone

A Listen and repeat the compound nouns above. Notice the stress pattern.

B Listen and complete the questions. Then ask and answer the questions with a partner.

1. Are there any good _____ near your home?
2. Is there a big _____ around here?
3. Are there any _____ outside this building?
4. Is there a _____ in this neighborhood?
5. Is there a good _____ near your home?
6. Are there any _____ around here?

Getting around

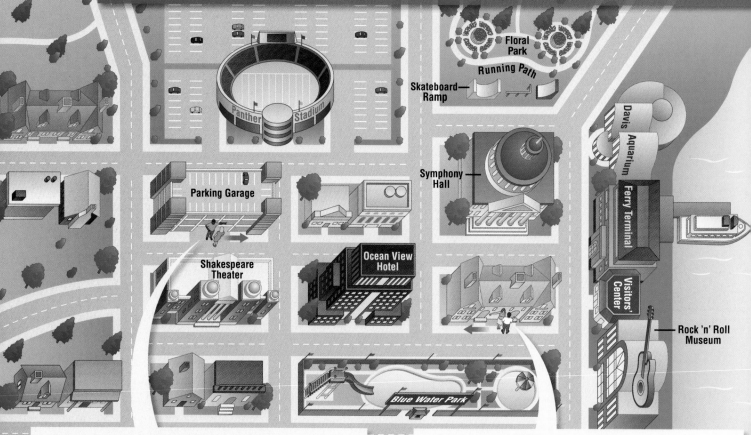

A Excuse me, could you give me directions to the Rock 'n' Roll Museum?

B Sure. Go straight ahead for two blocks. You're going to see a ferry terminal. Make a right and go down the street about a block. It's on the left.

C Are you lost? Can I help you?

D Yes, thanks. Can you tell me how to get to Panther Stadium?

C Sure. Go to the end of the next block, and turn right. Walk up two blocks. You can't miss it.

1 Building vocabulary

A Listen to the conversations, and follow the directions on the map. Then underline all the expressions for directions. Practice with a partner.

Figure it out → **B** Can you put these directions in order? First find your location on the map, and then find your destination.

You're just outside the parking garage. You ask:
"Could you tell me how to get to the aquarium?"

- [ ] The aquarium is going to be on your right.
- [ ] You're going to see a ferry terminal.
- [1] Go straight ahead for two blocks.
- [ ] Make a left.
- [ ] Walk up the street about one block.

You're in the Ocean View Hotel. You ask:
"Can you give me directions to Symphony Hall?"

- [ ] Then make a right.
- [ ] Turn left again at the corner, and walk up a block.
- [ ] It's right there, on the left.
- [ ] When you go out of the hotel, turn left.

2 Grammar *Offers and requests with Can and Could*

Offers	Requests
Can I help you?	**Can** you help me?
What **can** I do?	**Can** you tell me how to get to the aquarium?
How **can** I help?	**Could** you give me directions?

In conversation . . .

Can you . . . ? is more common than *Could you . . . ?* for requests. People use *Could you . . . ?* to make their requests more polite.

Can you . . .?

Could you . . .?

A Some people are asking for directions at the Visitors' Center on the map on page 56. Complete the questions and write directions for each person.

1. *A* _____ you tell me how to get to Panther Stadium?
   B Sure. Just go _____ .

2. *A* _____ you give me directions to the Shakespeare Theater? Is it far from here?
   B Uh, it's not far. Walk _____ .

3. *A* _____ you recommend a place to go running?
   B Let me think. There's a running path in Floral Park. Go _____ .

4. *A* _____ I help you?
   B Yes, thanks. Is this the right way to Blue Water Park?
   A Yes, just go _____ .

B *Pair work* Now take turns asking for and giving directions to the places above.

3 Listening and speaking *Finding your way around*

A Look at the map on page 56. Listen to the concierge at the Ocean View Hotel give directions to people. Where do they want to go? Number the places.

| the aquarium | the ferry terminal | the Rock 'n' Roll Museum | Panther Stadium |

About you

B *Pair work* Ask and answer questions about the neighborhood you are in. Use these questions, or think of your own.

▸ Could you recommend a cheap restaurant around here?
▸ Is there a place to go skateboarding or biking near here?
▸ Can you tell me how to get to the subway or to a bus stop?
▸ Could you give me directions to the nearest video arcade?

A **Could you recommend a cheap restaurant around here?**
B **Sure. Try Ann's Diner. When you leave the building, turn left. Then . . .**

4 Vocabulary notebook *Which way?*

See page 62 for a new way to log and learn vocabulary.

Excuse me?

1 Conversation strategy *Checking information*

A What are the best ways to check information? Choose two responses.

A *Excuse me. Is there a mall around here?*
B ☐ *Huh?* ☐ *A mall?* ☐ *Did you say a mall?*

Now listen. What is there to do near the hotel?

Concierge	**Hi. Can I help you?**
Kate	**Yes. What is there to do around here? Within walking distance.**
Concierge	**Within walking distance? Well, the Center Mall is a 15-minute walk from here.**
Kate	**Fifteen or fifty?**
Concierge	**Fifteen. They have a lot of good stores and movie theaters. Or if you want to go see a play, there's . . .**
Kate	**I'm sorry? A play? Um . . . no, I think a movie sounds better. Did you say the Center Mall?**
Concierge	**Yes, it's right down this street. The new John Woo movie is playing – I heard it's good.**
Kate	**Excuse me? The new what?**
Concierge	**The new John Woo movie. It got great reviews.**

Restaurant ↑
Meeting Rooms
← Parking

CONCIERGE

Notice how Kate and the concierge check information. They repeat words as a question or use "checking" expressions. Find examples in the conversation.

"It's a 15-minute walk from here."
"Fifteen or fifty?"

"Checking" expressions:
I'm sorry?
Excuse me?
Did you say . . . ?
What did you say?

B Match the questions with the checking responses. Then practice with a partner. Give your own answers.

1. Could you give me directions to the airport? __c__
2. Is there an Indonesian restaurant near here? _____
3. Do you have a number for a cab company? _____
4. Where is there a bookstore around here? _____
5. Are there any good concerts on this week? _____

a. Did you say Indian or Indonesian?
b. I'm sorry? Did you say a bookstore?
c. Sorry, what did you say? The airport?
d. Excuse me? Did you say cab?
e. Concerts, did you say?

SELF-STUDY
AUDIO CD
CD-ROM

2 *Strategy plus* "Echo" questions

In an "echo" question, you repeat something you heard, and you add a question word to check information you didn't hear.

The new John Woo movie is playing.

Excuse me? The new what?

Here are some more examples:

A The video arcade is on Beach Street.
B I'm sorry, it's *where*?

A It opens at 10:00.
B Excuse me? It opens at *what time*?

▶ **In conversation . . .**

When people ask others to repeat information, they say ***I'm sorry?*** more often than ***Excuse me?***

| | I'm sorry? |
| | Excuse me? |

A Complete the conversations with "echo" questions. Use the question words in the box. Then practice with a partner.

| how far | how much | ✓what | what kind | what time | where |

1. *A* There are lots of street performers in the city right now.
   B I'm sorry, there are a lot of _____what_____ ?
2. *A* There's a miniature golf course about 15 minutes away.
   B Excuse me, it's _____ ?
3. *A* The best outdoor pool around here is at Ocean Beach.
   B I'm sorry, it's _____ ?
4. *A* There are great gift shops in this neighborhood.
   B I'm sorry, there are _____ of shops?
5. *A* The movie theater opens at 10:15 a.m.
   B Excuse me, it opens at _____ ?
6. *A* Rides in the amusement park cost $5.
   B They cost _____ ?

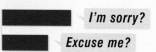

About you

B *Pair work* Student A: Tell a partner about a place you know well. Use the ideas above. Student B: Check the information you hear. Then change roles.

"There are some nice stores in this neighborhood." *"I'm sorry, there are some what?"*

3 *Listening* Tourist information

A 💿 Listen to the beginning of six conversations at a tourist-information desk. What do you think each person says next to check the information? Number the sentences.

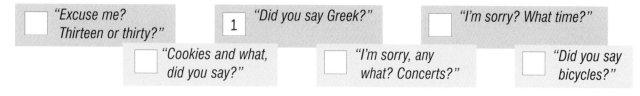

| | *"Excuse me? Thirteen or thirty?"* | **1** *"Did you say Greek?"* | | *"I'm sorry? What time?"* |

| | *"Cookies and what, did you say?"* | *"I'm sorry, any what? Concerts?"* | | *"Did you say bicycles?"* |

B 💿 Now listen to the complete conversations, and check your answers. What other information does the clerk give each person? Make notes. Then compare with a partner.

59

Exploring the city

1 Reading

A Are there any interesting places to walk around your city? Where are they? Can you go on a walking tour? Tell the class.

B Read these pages from a walking-tour guide. As you read, follow the tour on the map.

A Walking Tour of San Francisco's
CHINATOWN

San Francisco's Chinatown is the largest Chinese community on the West Coast of the U.S. and is now home to over 14,000 people. Chinese settlers came here as early as 1846, opening businesses near Portsmouth Square.

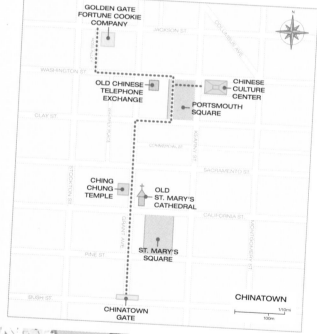

3. Across from the cathedral on California is **St. Mary's Square** – a quiet park with a statue of the Chinese revolutionary leader Sun Yat-sen.

4. Opposite the cathedral on Grant, the **Ching Chung Temple** welcomes visitors and has year-round guided tours.

5. Continue north on Grant, and turn right on Clay Street. Then turn left into **Portsmouth Square**, and watch local people play cards or Chinese chess.

6. Take the footbridge across Kearny Street to the **Chinese Culture Center**. Here there are exhibitions of Chinese and Chinese-American art, as well as a permanent display of Chinese musical instruments. It's well worth a visit.

7. Return to the square, and turn left onto Washington Street. On the left is the **Old Chinese Telephone Exchange**. Now a bank, the exchange opened in 1909. Operators had to speak English and five Chinese dialects.

1. The tour begins at the **Chinatown Gate** at the intersection of Bush Street and Grant Avenue. Walk north on Grant – a busy street of shops selling souvenirs, jewelry, artwork, furniture, cameras, and electronics.

2. At the corner of California and Grant, look around **Old St. Mary's Cathedral** (1891) and its display of historic photographs of 19th-century Chinatown.

8. Continue west on Washington, and turn right into Ross Alley. Near the end of the block is the **Golden Gate Fortune Cookie Company**, where you can sample the fortune cookies.

This is where your tour ends. We hope you enjoy your tour of San Francisco's Chinatown.

C Read the guide again, and answer the questions. Then compare with a partner.

1. Where can you do these things, according to the guide?
   a. look at old photographs
   b. listen to someone talk about a temple
   c. buy Chinese art
   d. eat a well-known dessert
2. Where is the best place to take interesting pictures, do you think?
3. Which three places would you like to see on this tour? Why?

2 *Talk about it* What are some of your favorite places?

Group work Discuss places in your town or city. Can you agree on the best place to do these things?

Is there . . .

► a good place to sit and watch people go by?
► a fun place to spend a rainy afternoon?
► a cheap (but good) place to eat?
► a quiet area to go for a walk or a jog?
► a good place to shop for electronic products?
► an interesting museum?
► a neighborhood with lots of cultural events?
► a neighborhood with lots of interesting nightlife?

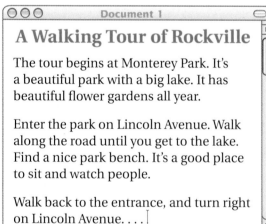

3 *Writing* A walking-tour guide

A Write a guide for a walking tour for an area in your city or town. Write about three different places. Give directions and explain why they are worth a visit.

```
○○○              Document 1
▲
  A Walking Tour of Rockville

  The tour begins at Monterey Park. It's
  a beautiful park with a big lake. It has
  beautiful flower gardens all year.

  Enter the park on Lincoln Avenue. Walk
  along the road until you get to the lake.
  Find a nice park bench. It's a good place
  to sit and watch people.

  Walk back to the entrance, and turn right
  on Lincoln Avenue. . . .|
▼
◄│►
```

Help note

Giving directions

The tour begins at _____ .
Turn right on _____ Street.
Return to . . . / Walk back to . . .
Walk north for two blocks.
Continue east on _____ Street.

North
West — East
South

B **Group work** Read your classmates' guides. Choose a tour you would like to take. Tell the group which tour you chose and why.

4 *Free talk* Summer fun

For more speaking practice, go to the back of the book.
Student A: See **Free talk 6A**. Student B: See **Free talk 6B**.

Vocabulary notebook

Which way?

Learning tip Drawing maps

Draw and label a map to help you remember directions.

Is there a bank around here?

People say **around here** 50 times more frequently than **near here**.

1 Use the map to number the directions to the bank below.

Directions

	Walk one more block.
	Turn right.
1	Walk up one block.
	Make a left.
	It's on the left, just past the post office.

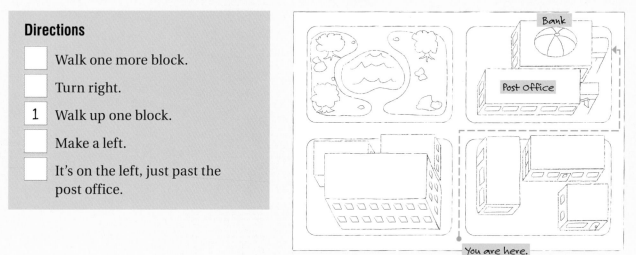

2 Now draw your own map. Show the way from your home or class to a place you often go to. Then write the directions to go with the map.

Directions from my _____ to _____

1. _____

   _____

2. _____

   _____

3. _____

   _____

4. _____

   _____

My map

On your own

Find a map of your town or city. Highlight the route from one place you know to another. Then write directions. Learn the directions.

1 Unscramble the questions.

Put the words in the correct order to make questions. Then ask and answer the questions with a partner.

1. doing / are / next weekend / what / you ?

   What are you doing next weekend?

2. after class / going to / you / go shopping / are ?

   _____

3. it / rain / tomorrow / going to / is ?

   _____

4. you / here / did / another city / from / move ?

   _____

5. last year / you / did / on vacation / go / where ?

   _____

6. what / your / in school / favorite / was / subject ?

   _____

7. are / a lot of / in / fun places / neighborhood / there / your ?

   _____

2 Can you complete this conversation?

Complete the conversation. Use the words and expressions in the box. Use capital letters where necesssary. Then practice with a partner.

where	✓is there a	I mean	was born	until	did you say	I'm not sure
what	him	and everything	one	my grandfather	actually	

A _Is there a_ good music store around here?

B There's _____ on the corner of Fifth and Oak.

A It's _____ ?

B On Fifth Avenue, _____ , Sixth Avenue, and Oak.

A _____ Sixth Avenue? A couple of blocks away?

B Yeah. They have all kinds of music, and you can watch music videos and do karaoke _____ .

A You can do _____ ?

B Karaoke. I went last week. Well, _____ , I didn't go inside, but it looks great. Do you want to go?

A Now? _____ . What time does it close?

B It doesn't close _____ midnight.

A Oh, OK. I can get _____ a video for his birthday.

B You buy _____ music videos? How old is he?

A Well, he _____ in 1945, so how old is that?

B I don't know. I never could do math.

3 *What can you remember?*

A Add five words to each category, and compare with a partner. Ask questions to find out more information.

"Are you going to celebrate Halloween?"   *"Yes, I am. You too? Are you going to have a party, or . . . ?"*

Events you are going to celebrate this year	Important dates for you	Places in town you go to often	Subjects you're never going to study
Halloween	May 1st – my birthday	the bank	biology

B Choose a category and survey your class or group. Report your findings to the class.

"Most of us are going to celebrate Halloween."   *"Nobody is going to send a Valentine's card."*

4 *Get it right!*

A Can you complete these questions? Use the words in the box.

walk	1. What's your city, I mean, your _____ like?
best	2. Are you going to any birthday parties, I mean, _____ this year?
neighborhood	3. Can you give me directions to a bank around here? I mean, a _____ ?
weddings	4. When did you learn to swim? I mean, when did you learn to _____ ?
cash machine	5. What was your worst, I mean, _____ subject in school?

B *Pair work* Take turns asking the questions. Use "vague" expressions in your answers. Check your partner's answers with "echo" questions.

A What's your city, I mean, your neighborhood like?
B Well, I like it. There's a lot to do. We have a lot of cafés and restaurants and everything.
A I'm sorry. A lot of what?

5 *Do you know your city?*

Pair work Write directions from your school to three places nearby. Then trade papers. Can your partner guess the places?

1. Cross the street, turn left, and walk up three blocks. This place is on the right, next to the bank. What is it?

1. The music store.

Self-check

How sure are you about these areas? Circle the percentages.

grammar
20% 40% 60% 80% 100%
vocabulary
20% 40% 60% 80% 100%
conversation strategies
20% 40% 60% 80% 100%

. . . .

Study plan

What do you want to review? Circle the lessons.

grammar
4A 4B 5A 5B 6A 6B
vocabulary
4A 4B 5A 5B 6A 6B
conversation strategies
4C 5C 6C

Free talk 1   *Me too!*

Class activity First write your answers to these questions. Then ask your classmates the questions. Find people who have things in common with you. Write their names.

	My answers	**Classmates with the same answers**
1. What's your favorite color?	blue	Kumiko
2. What food do you hate most?		
3. What sport do you play?		
4. How many sisters do you have?		
5. How many hours a week do you watch TV?		
6. What's your favorite day of the week?		
7. How often do you have dinner with your family?		
8. What do you usually wear on weekends?		
9. What time do you usually get up on Sundays?		

A **What's your favorite color, Kumiko?**

B **Blue. How about you?**

A **Me too. All my clothes are blue and . . .**

Free talk 2   *The game of likes and dislikes*

1 Think of one thing for each section of the chart. You have three minutes to write in your answers.

I enjoy watching _____ . (a sport)	**I can't play** _____ . (a sport)	**I'm good at** _____ . (an activity)
I think everybody loves _____ . (a type of music)	**I'd like to play the** _____ . (a musical instrument)	**I want to learn (to)** _____ . (a hobby)
I'm interested in reading about _____ . (a topic)	**I can't stand talking about** _____ . (a topic)	**I hate watching** _____ . (a type of TV show)

2 Group work Compare your charts. If anyone in the group has the same answer as you, score one point. Who scores the most points?

A **OK, I enjoy watching golf. How about you?**

B **I enjoy watching ice-skating.**

C **I do too! So we each get one point.**

D **I enjoy watching ice-skating, too, so I get a point, too!**

Score box:

A	B	C	D
	1	1	1

1 Pair work Read the questions and possible answers to your partner. Circle your partner's answers. Then change roles.

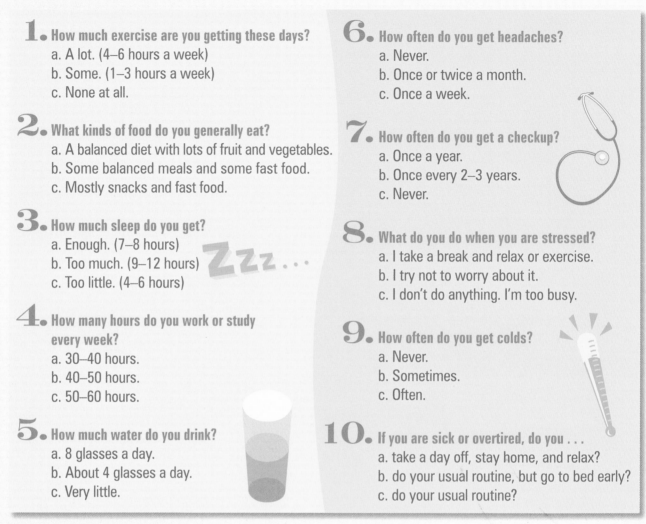

1. How much exercise are you getting these days?
   a. A lot. (4–6 hours a week)
   b. Some. (1–3 hours a week)
   c. None at all.

2. What kinds of food do you generally eat?
   a. A balanced diet with lots of fruit and vegetables.
   b. Some balanced meals and some fast food.
   c. Mostly snacks and fast food.

3. How much sleep do you get?
   a. Enough. (7–8 hours)
   b. Too much. (9–12 hours)
   c. Too little. (4–6 hours)

4. How many hours do you work or study every week?
   a. 30–40 hours.
   b. 40–50 hours.
   c. 50–60 hours.

5. How much water do you drink?
   a. 8 glasses a day.
   b. About 4 glasses a day.
   c. Very little.

6. How often do you get headaches?
   a. Never.
   b. Once or twice a month.
   c. Once a week.

7. How often do you get a checkup?
   a. Once a year.
   b. Once every 2–3 years.
   c. Never.

8. What do you do when you are stressed?
   a. I take a break and relax or exercise.
   b. I try not to worry about it.
   c. I don't do anything. I'm too busy.

9. How often do you get colds?
   a. Never.
   b. Sometimes.
   c. Often.

10. If you are sick or overtired, do you . . .
   a. take a day off, stay home, and relax?
   b. do your usual routine, but go to bed early?
   c. do your usual routine?

2 Figure out your partner's score. Give 3 points for each **(a)** answer, 2 points for each **(b)** answer, and 1 point for each **(c)** answer. Add them together for the total. Then read the health profile to your partner.

a	_____	x 3 =	_____
b	_____	x 2 =	_____
c	_____	x 1 =	_____
		=	_____ *Total*

Health Profiles

24 to 30 points
You are taking very good care of your health. That's good news! If you have any **(b)** or **(c)** answers, then you can still improve. See if you can make one improvement each month.

17 to 23 points
You are taking pretty good care of your health, but you can do better. If you want to feel really good and have a lot of energy, choose two things to improve each month. You can do it!

10 to 16 points
You are not taking good care of your health. You need to change your diet and your lifestyle. Sleep and exercise are very important, and so is relaxation. Choose three things to improve each month and start today!

1 **Group work** Create a new special day or festival. You can use the ideas given or make up anything you want! Complete these sentences about your new event.

1. Our new festival or special day is called _____ . (*name*)
2. It's going to be on _____ . (*date*)
3. There's going to be _____ and _____ . (*events*)
4. Everyone is going to _____ . (*activity*)
5. Everyone is going to eat _____ . (*food*)
6. People are going to buy _____ . (*items*)
7. Nobody is going to _____ . (*activity*)
8. It's going to be _____ . ("*fun*," "*interesting*," . . .)

Grandma's Day

Chocolate Festival

No-Homework Day!

Get-Up-Late Week

National Skip-Class Day

2 **Class activity** Ask three classmates from other groups questions about their new festivals and special days. Take notes.

A *What's your new festival called?*
B *It's called "Laugh-a-Lot Day," and it's going to be on March 8th.*

3 Choose one festival that you'd like to celebrate. Tell the class why.

"I'd like to celebrate Laugh-a-Lot Day because people are going to tell jokes all day."

Pair work Student A: Read the brochure about Seasons Resort. Your partner has a brochure for Breezes Resort. Take turns asking questions. Do the resorts have the same attractions? Decide which resort you would like to go to.

"Is there a water park at Breezes Resort?"   *"A water park? No, there isn't, but there's an . . ."*

It's fun, fun, *fun* at Seasons Resort!

Sports:	**Splashaway Water Park** – Pools and water fun for the whole family!
	Crazy Golf – Miniature golf for all ages!
Dining:	Over 50 fast-food restaurants for eating out!
Shopping:	Outlet mall just 30 minutes away. Over 200 brand-name stores!
Movies:	3 multiplex cinemas with 20 screens. See all the latest movies!
Entertainment:	Nightly concerts. Top international bands!
	Fun Plaza – Video arcade, bowling, and disco roller-skating!
	Waxworks Museum – See your favorite celebrities!

Class activity Ask your classmates questions about their childhood. Write notes about each person.

Find someone who . . .	Name	Notes
1. was born at home.	_____	_____
2. didn't like playing outside.	_____	_____
3. wasn't good at music.	_____	_____
4. liked to play board games.	_____	_____
5. always had bruised knees.	_____	_____
6. was on a sports or an athletics team.	_____	_____
7. changed schools two or three times.	_____	_____
8. had a teddy bear.	_____	_____
9. got into trouble a lot.	_____	_____
10. liked to eat vegetables.	_____	_____

"Were you born at home?"   *"Did you like playing outside?"*

Free talk 6B   *Summer fun*

Pair work Student B: Read the brochure about Breezes Resort. Your partner has a brochure for Seasons Resort. Take turns asking questions. Do the resorts have the same attractions? Decide which resort you would like to go to.

"Are there any concerts at Seasons Resort?"   *"Let's see. Um, yes. There are . . ."*

Something for everyone
at Breezes Resort!

Sports: Sports center with tennis, badminton, and racketball courts.
Olympic-size indoor and outdoor swimming pools.
Nine-hole public golf course. Open all year.

Dining: Fine dining at 15 international restaurants with world-famous chefs!

Shopping: European-style shopping street with designer boutiques and antiques.

Movies: Arts Cinema features foreign films in original versions with subtitles.

Entertainment: Free concerts daily in Breezes Garden – classical or jazz.
Sculpture Park with works from all around the world!
Summer Theater – see plays in the Breezes tent every evening!

Unit 1

A *Track 1* Listen to the conversation on page 6. Eve and Chris are talking outside a club.

B *Track 2* Listen to the rest of their conversation. Choose the right answer. Circle *a* or *b*.

1. How long is Eve in New York?
   a. For the weekend.   b. For the week.

2. Who has two free tickets?
   a. Chris.   b. Eve.

3. Who are the tickets for?
   a. Eve and her brother.   b. Eve and her friend.

4. Where is Eve's friend from?
   a. New York City.   b. Miami.

5. Why is her friend in the coffee shop?
   a. He's cold.   b. He's hungry.

6. When Chris says, "Oh. OK," how does he feel?
   a. Happy.   b. Disappointed.

Unit 2

A *Track 3* Listen to the conversation on page 16. Matt and Sarah are talking about hobbies.

B *Track 4* Listen to the rest of their conversation.
Check (✓) true or false for each sentence.

	True	False
1. Matt likes to take photos of people.	☐	☐
2. Matt uses his computer to change his photos.	☐	☐
3. Sarah says Matt's photos look like paintings.	☐	☐
4. Sometimes Matt sells his photos.	☐	☐
5. Matt gives Sarah a photo of some teacups.	☐	☐
6. Sarah wants to make a sweater for Matt.	☐	☐

Unit 3

A *Track 5* Listen to the conversation on page 26. Adam and Yuki are talking in the library.

B *Track 6* Listen to the rest of their conversation. Make these sentences true
for Adam and Yuki. Circle the correct words.

1. Sometimes Adam **eats** / **sleeps** in the library during the day.
2. Adam puts his head on his **books** / **arms** and goes to sleep.
3. He usually sleeps for about **an hour** / **half an hour**.
4. **An alarm clock** / **A friend** wakes Adam up in time for class.
5. Adam's clock doesn't make any noise because **it's very small** / **it vibrates**.

Unit 4

A *Track 7* Listen to the conversation on page 38. Ray and Tina are talking about a festival.

B *Track 8* Listen to the rest of their conversation. Check (✓) true or false for each sentence.

	True	False
1. The festival has dance shows on two nights.	☐	☐
2. There are songs and dances from different parts of Mexico.	☐	☐
3. Tina wants to go to the festival on Sunday.	☐	☐
4. Tina and Ray decide to go to the dance show in the evening.	☐	☐
5. They decide to go to the children's parade in the morning.	☐	☐
6. Tina and Ray plan to wear costumes all afternoon.	☐	☐

Unit 5

A *Track 9* Listen to the conversation on page 48. Ben is telling Jessica a story.

B *Track 10* Listen to the rest of their conversation. Complete the sentences. Circle *a* or *b*.

1. Jessica lived _____ the school.
   a. down the street from
   b. an hour from

2. Jessica usually _____ home from school.
   a. walked
   b. took the bus

3. She wanted to ride the bus because _____ .
   a. she didn't like to walk
   b. her friends took the bus

4. The bus driver drove Jessica _____ .
   a. back to the school
   b. to her house

Unit 6

A *Track 11* Listen to the conversation on page 58. Kate is talking to the concierge at a hotel.

B *Track 12* Listen to the rest of their conversation. Choose the right answer. Circle *a* or *b*.

1. What is Kate's hobby?
   a. Fishing.   b. Scuba diving.

2. What does the aquarium have?
   a. A good restaurant.   b. A good gift shop.

3. Where is the aquarium?
   a. On First Avenue and River Street.
   b. On First Avenue by the river.

4. How long does it take to walk there?
   a. About forty-five minutes.
   b. About five minutes.

5. What does Kate decide to do?
   a. Swim in the pool.
   b. Read by the pool.

Unit 1

Chris So, your brother's in Miami 305? Who's your brother?
Eve This is him, right here.
Chris Wow. He's great. You know, I'm a really big fan. The band's from Miami, right?
Eve Yeah. How did you guess!
Chris So, are you from Miami, too?
Eve Yeah. I'm just in New York for the weekend.
Chris Really? Does your brother know you're here?
Eve Oh, sure. I have free tickets.
Chris Free tickets? That's great! Um . . . how many do you have? I mean, do you have an extra ticket?
Eve Actually, no. Sorry. I only have two – a ticket for me and a ticket for my friend.
Chris Your friend?
Eve Yeah, a friend from Miami. He's across the street in the coffee shop. It's too cold for him out here!
Chris Oh. OK.

Unit 2

Sarah Hey, Matt. Do you have time to show me your photos?
Matt Sure. Just give me a minute. . . .
Sarah So, what kind of photos do you take? Do you take pictures of people?
Matt Um, no, not really. I like to take pictures of things . . . you know, things around the house or outside.
Sarah Hmm. That's interesting.
Matt Yeah. Then I download them on my computer and change the colors and things like that. Look. These are pictures of some teacups.
Sarah Oh, wow. They're beautiful. Huh! They look like paintings! Do you ever sell them?
Matt Oh, no. They're not that good! But if you want, I can give you a photo for your office.
Sarah Really? I love this picture of the bicycles.
Matt Sure. I can frame it and everything.
Sarah Thanks, Matt. You know, maybe I can make you a sweater or something.
Matt Oh, I'd love that. Thanks.

Unit 3

Adam Well, I often take a nap during the day.
Yuki You do? Where?
Adam Uh . . . well, sometimes I sleep here in the library.
Yuki Right here? No way! How do you do that?
Adam Well, if I'm really tired, I find a quiet desk, and I just put my head on my books and go to sleep. . . .
Yuki Are you serious? How long do you sleep?
Adam Oh, usually for about an hour.
Yuki Do you wake up in time for class?
Adam Oh, yeah. I have an alarm clock.
Yuki An alarm clock? In the library? You're kidding!
Adam It doesn't ring. It vibrates, so it doesn't make any noise.
Yuki Oh, that's good. Um, anyway, can I ask you a question about our math homework?
Adam *(yawns)* Excuse me. Oh, sure.
Yuki Well, I don't really understand this one problem. . . . Where is it? . . . Oh, here it is. Yeah. Adam? Adam?

Unit 4

Ray Well, you know, there's dancing, too. . . . Spanish and Mexican dancing. They have special shows and everything.
Tina Oh, really? I love dance shows. When are they?
Ray Let's see. . . . They have shows on . . . Thursday, Friday, and Saturday nights. What do you think? Do you want to go?
Tina Um, maybe. What's in the show exactly?
Ray Well, . . . there's Spanish flamenco dancing. And songs and dances and things from different parts of Mexico.
Tina Huh. That sounds great. Um . . . OK. Let's go to the fiesta on Saturday. We can go to the music and dance show in the evening. . . .
Ray Yeah, let's do that. And we can see the children's parade in the morning.
Tina Right. And eat tacos and stuff all afternoon.

Unit 5

Jessica That's funny. You know, something similar happened to me.
Ben Really?
Jessica Yeah. Our house was right next to the school, I mean, right down the street, so I just had to walk a few minutes and I was home.
Ben Wow. My bus ride took an hour. You were lucky.
Jessica Yeah, but I always wanted to take the school bus. All my friends went home on the bus, and it looked kind of fun.
Ben Right.
Jessica So anyway, one day I just got on the bus with the other kids.
Ben You did?
Jessica Yeah. I don't know why. And we drove around, and all the other kids went home, and then the bus driver asked me, "Where do *you* live? Did I miss your stop?"
Ben How old were you?
Jessica Oh, six or seven. No, wait, maybe I was eight. Anyway, I said, "No. I live near the school." So he drove back.
Ben He drove you all the way back to the school?
Jessica Yeah. I was on the bus for hours. My mom was so worried.
Ben Oh, yeah.
Jessica She was really mad at me! But I just wanted to ride the bus.
Ben Oh, that's funny.

Unit 6

Kate So, what else is there to do? I mean, if I don't go to a movie.
Concierge Well, the aquarium is interesting. . . .
Kate Oh, did you say aquarium? I love looking at fish. My hobby is scuba diving.
Concierge Well, the aquarium's very nice. It has a good restaurant, too. It's on First Avenue and River Street.
Kate I'm sorry, it's where? First Avenue and . . . ?
Concierge First Avenue and River Street. It's on the corner. You can't miss it.
Kate Yeah. That sounds interesting. And it's within walking distance?
Concierge Well, yes, . . . if you like to walk.
Kate How long does it take to get there?
Concierge About 40 or 45 minutes.
Kate Oh, 45 minutes? Huh. . . . You know, I think I just want to sit by the pool and read. But thanks for your help!
Concierge You're welcome. Have a great afternoon!

Answer key
Unit 1 1. a 2. b 3. b 4. b 5. a 6. b
Unit 2 1. False 2. True 3. True 4. False 5. False 6. True
Unit 3 1. sleeps 2. books 3. an hour 4. An alarm clock 5. it vibrates

Unit 4 1. False 2. True 3. False 4. True 5. True 6. False
Unit 5 1. a 2. a 3. b 4. a
Unit 6 1. b 2. a 3. a 4. a 5. b

Illustration credits

Photography credits

Text credits

TOUCHSTONE

SUSAN RIVERS
GEORGIANA FARNOAGA

2A

WORKBOOK

CAMBRIDGE
UNIVERSITY PRESS

Contents

Unit 1 Making friends

Lesson A Getting to know you

1 About you 1

Grammar and vocabulary

A Complete the chart with the words in the box.

class	fun	movies	only child	TV
college	major	✓neighborhood	parents	

Home and family	School	Free time
neighborhood		

B Answer the questions with your own information. Use short answers.

1. Are you an only child? _Yes, I am._ 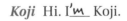 _No, I'm not._
2. Is your neighborhood quiet? _____
3. Do you live with your parents? _____
4. Do you have a big TV? _____
5. Do you and your friends go to college? _____
6. Are you a French major? _____
7. Does your best friend like action movies? _____
8. Is your English class fun? _____

2 You and me

Grammar Complete the conversation with the verb *be*. Use contractions where possible.

Koji Hi. I'_m_ Koji.

Isabel Hi. I _____ Isabel. Where _____ you from, Koji?

Koji I _____ from Japan. How about you?

Isabel Mexico, from Monterrey.

Koji Oh, my friends Manuel and Rosa _____ from Mexico, too.

Isabel Really? _____ your friends here now?

Koji No, they _____ not. Uh, I guess they _____ late.

Isabel _____ the teacher here?

Koji Yes, she _____ . She _____ over there.

Isabel She looks nice. What _____ her name?

Koji I think it _____ Ms. Barnes.

2

3 *I'm Rudy.*

Grammar   Answer the questions. Write another piece of information.

1. Is Rudy from San Francisco?
   <u>No, he's not. He's from Los Angeles.</u>

2. Are his friends English majors?
   _____

3. Do his friends study in the evening?
   _____

4. Is he from a large family?
   _____

4 *About you 2*

Grammar and vocabulary   Unscramble the questions. Then answer the questions with your own information.

1. name / What's / first / your ? <u>What's your first name?</u>
   _____

2. full-time / a / Do / have / you / job ? _____
   _____

3. live / best friend / Does / your / nearby ? _____
   _____

4. weekends / What / do / on / you / do ? _____
   _____

5. Where / you / for fun / go / do ? _____
   _____

6. teacher / your / like / What's ? _____
   _____

1 What doesn't belong?

Vocabulary Circle the word that doesn't belong in each group.

1. apples (butter) mangoes strawberries
2. CD jacket jeans sweater
3. black color green red

4. baseball basketball singing volleyball
5. cat dog fish pet
6. dessert juice milk water

2 We're the same.

Grammar Respond to the statements with *too* or *either*.

1. I'm a soccer fan.
   I am too.

2. I can't stand doing the laundry.
   _____

3. I can sing karaoke all night.
   _____

4. I'm not a good cook.
   _____

5. I don't like shopping.
   _____

6. I love to swim in cold water.
   _____

3 First date

Grammar
and
vocabulary

**Complete the conversations with the expressions in the box.
Use each expression only once.**

✓I am too.	I do too.	I can too.	Me too.	Really?
I'm not either.	I don't either.	I can't either.	Me neither.	

David You know, I'm always nervous on first dates.
Lesley ___I am too.___
David So, tell me about yourself, Lesley. What do you like to do?
Lesley Well, I go to rock concerts.
David _____ I'm a big fan of U2.
Lesley _____ They're my favorite group. I mean, I can listen to their music for hours.
David _____ Do you have all their CDs?
Lesley No, I don't. I don't have *All That You Can't Leave Behind*.
David _____ But I want to buy it.

Later
Lesley What do you on the weekends?
        I mean, do you eat out a lot?
David No. I don't usually go to restaurants.
Lesley _____ I like to eat at home.
David Oh, are you a good cook?
Lesley Um, not really.
David _____ But I like to cook.
Lesley Do you ever cook Italian food?
David Sure. But I'm allergic to cheese, so I can't eat pizza.
Lesley _____ I'm allergic to cheese, too!
David That's amazing! We have a lot in common.
        Do you like sports?
Lesley Uh, no, not at all.
David _____ I'm a big sports fan. I watch sports all weekend.
Lesley Huh. I can't stand sports.

4 About you

Grammar
and
vocabulary

Respond to these statements so they are true for you.

1. *A* I always eat chocolate for dinner.
   B ___I do too. or Me too. or Really? I don't.___

2. *A* I'm not a baseball fan.
   B _____

3. *A* I can't drive.
   B _____

4. *A* I don't have a pet.
   B _____

5. *A* I'm allergic to bananas.
   B _____

6. *A* I can cook Italian food.
   B _____

Do you come here a lot?

1 Starting a conversation

Complete the conversations with the conversation starters in the box.

Is this your first English class here? You look really nice today. That's a beautiful jacket.
Hey, I don't know you. Do you live around here? Boy, the food is great. And this cake is really wonderful.
Is it me, or is it kind of noisy in here? ✓Ooh, it's cold. Can I close the window?

1. *A* <u>Ooh, it's cold. Can I close the window?</u>
   B Sorry, I just opened it. I'm a little warm, actually.

2. *A* _____
   B Thanks. Actually, it's from China.

3. *A* _____
   B Thank you. It's my grandmother's recipe.

4. *A* _____
   B Yes, it is. What about you?

5. *A* _____
   B Yeah, it's pretty loud! Is this your first time here?

6. *A* _____
   B Uh, no, I don't. I'm actually visiting from Guadalajara.

2 *Um, actually, . . .*

Circle the best response for each conversation starter.

1. I don't know anyone here. Do you?
   a. Um, actually, I know everybody.
   b. Actually, I don't know her.

2. So, are you British?
   a. Actually, where are you from?
   b. I'm Australian, actually.

3. Boy, it's hot today.
   a. Actually, I think it's OK.
   b. Well, actually, I do.

4. I like your jacket. Is it new?
   a. Actually, I like them, too.
   b. No, it's my sister's, actually.

5. This TV show is really interesting.
   a. It's a movie, actually.
   b. Actually, it was my grandfather's.

6. Do you work around here?
   a. No, I have a job, actually.
   b. Actually, I'm a full-time student.

7. It's a beautiful day. I love warm weather.
   a. You do, actually.
   b. Actually, I kind of like cold weather.

8. The bus is really late today.
   a. It's late every day, actually.
   b. Actually, it is late.

3 *First day of class*

Imagine it's the first day of English class. Respond to each conversation starter.

1. I don't know anyone here.   Me neither. By the way, I'm James.

2. This is a really big class.

3. Is it warm in here, or is it me?

4. Do you have a dictionary?

5. Are you a friend of Meg's?

6. I really like your cell phone.

7. Our teacher is really cool.

Making conversation

1 Getting together

A Look at the title of the article. Check (✓) the activities you think are in the article.

☐ do aerobics ☐ go shopping ☐ play tennis
☐ exercise at the gym ☐ join a club ☐ take a dance class
☐ get together and talk ☐ listen to music ☐ watch a movie

B Read the article. How many of your guesses in part A are correct?

World of Friends

Friends are important to all of us. They share our good days and our bad days. They are interested in us and our problems. But how do you make new friends? Here are some suggestions.

When you meet new people, find out what you have in common. Ask questions like, "What do you do in your free time?" or "What do you like to do on the weekends?" If you have things in common, you can do those activities together. It's fun to share your favorite activities with someone. If you both like movies, make a date to watch a movie. Or simply plan to get together one evening and talk – you don't have to spend money or go out to expensive places. Just spend time together.

But how can you meet new people? Think about your interests and the things you like to do. Do you have a hobby? Well, join a club. Do you want to learn to dance? Then sign up for a dance class. Start a conversation with people you meet at these places – you already have something in common.

When you start conversations with people, smile and be friendly. Make eye contact and don't forget to give compliments. People love to hear that they look nice or that you like their things, so be positive. Always listen to what the other person says, and ask follow-up questions.

When you make new friends, don't forget your old friends! Introduce your new friends to your old friends, too. After all, the more, the merrier!

C Read the article again. Match the two parts of each sentence.

1. Friends are important because __g__
2. Ask questions about general things _____
3. It's good to find out _____
4. It's not important to _____
5. Join clubs or take classes _____
6. Listen to the other person, _____
7. People love to hear _____

a. when you meet new people.
b. spend money – just spend time together.
c. and encourage him or her to talk.
d. nice things about themselves.
e. what activities you both like.
f. to meet people and make new friends.
g. they are interested in us and our problems.

2 Suggestions, please!

Writing **A** Read this e-mail to Marcy, the editor of *Friends* magazine, and her reply.
Correct the punctuation.

○○○ e-mail ⊖
dear marcy
what can I do i like to go out and do fun things
but I don't know how to meet new people my
friend says join a gym he's right but I don't like
to exercise
ben
dear ben
what are your hobbies take up a new sport or
hobby start conversations with people talk about
general topics
marcy

○○○ e-mail ⊖
Dear Marcy,
What can I do?

B Read these questions. Write three suggestions for each question.

1. *Dave* I'd like to make friends, but I don't know how. Do you have any suggestions?

_____

_____

_____

2. *Niki* I feel shy around new people. How can I improve my conversation skills?

_____

_____

_____

Unit 1 Progress chart

Mark the boxes below to rate your progress. ☑ = I know how to . . . ? = I need to review how to . . .	To review, go back to these pages in the Student's Book.
Grammar ☐ make statements with the simple present and with present of *be* ☐ ask questions with the simple present and present of *be* ☐ use *too* and *either* to agree	2, 3, 4, and 5 2 and 3 4 and 5
Vocabulary ☐ name words to describe lifestyle, home and family, and work and studies	2 and 3
Conversation strategies ☐ start conversations when meeting someone for the first time ☐ use *actually* to give and "correct" information	6 and 7 7
Writing ☐ use correct punctuation	9

Unit 2 Interests

1 What do they like to do?

Grammar : Complete the sentences. Use the correct forms of the verbs in the box.

cook	dance	draw	play	✓read	work out

1. Pam and Victor aren't interested in <u>reading</u> books. They both prefer <u>to read</u> magazines. They really enjoy <u>reading</u> fashion magazines.

2. Ian would like _____ every day. He doesn't like _____ in the gym at all. He enjoys _____ at home with a video.

3. Sun Hee can't _____ now. She's interested in _____ and would like _____ the tango.

4. Tom isn't good at _____ people. He can't _____ people at all, but he can _____ animals very well.

5. Amy and Dave usually like _____ , but they hate _____ Italian food. They prefer _____ Chinese food.

6. Erica can't _____ the guitar very well. She enjoys _____ the guitar, but she's not very good at _____ it.

2 At home

Grammar

Complete the conversation. Use the correct form of the verbs in the box.

bowl	go	ski	try
✓exercise	play	swim	watch

Linda You and I watch too much TV. We need some exercise.

James I know, but I don't really enjoy __exercising__ .

Linda But you like _____ tennis, right?

James Yeah, but these days I prefer _____ tennis on TV.

Linda How about bowling? We can both _____ .

James Yeah, but it's always pretty noisy.

Linda I guess you're right.

James Well, you're good at _____ . And the pool is nearby.

Linda But it's always crowded.

James Oh, I know! We both like _____ .

Linda Actually, I can't stand the cold and snow.

James Really? Well, are you interested in _____ something new?

Linda Sure. I'd like _____ to the new Thai restaurant in our neighborhood.

James Great idea, Linda. Let's talk about exercise tomorrow.

3 About you

Grammar and vocabulary

Answer the questions. Add more information.

1. **A** What are you good at?

   B Well, I'm pretty good at learning languages. I can speak Portuguese and French.

2. **A** Would you like to play a musical instrument?

   B _____

3. **A** What movie do you want to see?

   B _____

4. **A** Is there anything you really hate doing?

   B _____

5. **A** What activities do you enjoy doing on the weekends?

   B _____

6. **A** What are you bad at?

   B _____

Music

1 All kinds of music

Vocabulary   Look at the pictures. Write the type of music.

1. ___folk music___   2. _____   3. _____   4. _____

5. _____   6. _____   7. _____   8. _____

2 What's new?

Grammar   Complete Kevin's e-mail with the correct pronouns.

○○○   **e-mail**

Hi Sam,

Guess what! My new job is at a music store. You know __me__ (it / me) – I love listening to music. It's a great job, and I really like _____ (him / it).

So, what's cool right now? Well, the new Green Day CD is amazing! They're my favorite band. Do you like _____ (her / them)? My friends like Usher. Actually, almost _____ (everybody / nobody) I know is an Usher fan. But I don't really care for _____ (you / him). Gretchen Wilson is cool. Do you know _____ (her / us)? You like country music, right? You know, I actually kind of like _____ (it / them) now.

Oh, did I tell you? I'm in a band with my friends from the music store. They're really great. I want you to meet _____ (him / them). We play hip-hop. But my family never comes to listen to _____ (them / us) because (everyone / no one) _____ in my family likes hip-hop! But that's OK.

What's new with you? Write soon.

Kevin

---

3 Talking about music

Grammar · **Complete the questions with object pronouns. Then answer the questions.**

1. *A* Gwen Stefani is a great singer. She's pretty, too.
   Do you like __her__?
   B __Yes, I do. She's amazing._____

2. *A* You know Justin Timberlake, right? I think he's great.
   What do you think of _____?
   B _____

3. *A* You know, I'm not a fan of rap. How about you?
   Do you ever listen to _____?
   B _____

4. *A* Hey, the band Outkast performed on TV last night.
   They're really cool. Do you know _____?
   B _____

5. *A* My mom and dad love Sarah Chang. She's their
   favorite violinist. Do your parents like _____?
   B _____

6. *A* Do you like Latin music? Jeff and I have tickets for the
   Shakira concert. Do you want to go with _____?
   B _____

7. *A* I don't usually like country music, but I love the Dixie
   Chicks. Do you know _____?
   B _____

Gwen Stefani

Outkast

4 About you

Grammar and vocabulary · **Answer the questions using object pronouns. Then give more information.**

1. Do you like Alicia Keys? __Yes, I like her a lot. She has some great songs._____
2. What do you think of the Rolling Stones? _____
3. Do you like Mariah Carey? _____
4. Do you listen to pop music very often? _____
5. What do you think of folk music? _____
6. Do you and your friends ever go to concerts? _____
7. What do you think of Marc Anthony? _____
8. Do you know the band Destiny's Child? _____

I really like making things.

1 Saying no

Conversation strategies

Complete the conversations with the sentences in the box.

Um, no. He's lazy and just watches TV all day.   ✓ Not really. My mom knitted it for me last year.
Actually, no. My sister got it at the bakery.   No, but he has a big cap collection.
Well, no. I prefer to make peanut butter cookies.   No. I'm not really good with my hands.
Um, no, he just plays computer games!   Not really. He does crossword puzzles, though.

1. *Jenny*   I really like your sweater. Is it new?

   Keiko   <u>Not really. My mom knitted it for me last year.</u>

   Jenny   Can you knit or crochet?

   Keiko   _____ But I bake a little.

   Jenny   Oh, did you make this cake?

   Keiko   _____

   But I like to make cookies sometimes.

   Jenny   Me too. Do you ever make chocolate chip cookies?

   Keiko   _____

   My new boyfriend loves them!

2. *Mike*   I want to buy a Yankees baseball cap for my brother.

   Greg   Why? Is it his birthday?

   Mike   _____

   Does your brother collect anything?

   Greg   My brother? _____

   Mike   Really? Does he have *any* hobbies?

   Greg   _____

   Mike   Oh, yeah? My brother is on the computer all the time.

   Greg   Oh, does he do computer graphics?

   Mike   _____

2 No, not really.

Conversation strategies

Complete the responses to make them more friendly.

1. *A* Are you into the Internet?

   B Not really. <u>I don't have a computer.</u>

2. *A* What a great photo! Are you interested
   in photography?

   B No. _____

3. *A* I really enjoy my piano lessons. Would
   you like to learn the piano?

   B Um, no. _____

4. *A* Look at these flowers. They're so
   beautiful. Do you enjoy gardening?

   B Well, not really. _____

2 Susan's lifestyle

Grammar **Look at the picture. Then answer the questions with the correct form of the verbs in the box.**

do karate	eat fruit	play tennis
✓drink water	exercise	try to lose weight

1. What is Susan doing now to stay healthy?

   a. <u>She's drinking water.</u>

   b. _____

   c. _____

2. What else does she do to stay healthy?

   a. _____

   b. _____

   c. _____

3 About you

Grammar and vocabulary **Are these sentences true or false for you? Write *T* (true) or *F* (false). Then correct the false statements.**

1. <u>F</u> I'm drinking a lot of milk these days.

   <u>I'm not drinking a lot of milk these days. I'm drinking a lot of soda.</u>

2. _____ My best friend eats junk food every other day.

   _____

3. _____ I'm not taking any classes right now.

   _____

4. _____ I sleep for five hours a night.

   _____

5. _____ My friends have a lot of stress in their lives.

   _____

6. _____ My family doesn't get any exercise at all.

   _____

Aches and pains

1 What's the matter?

Vocabulary **A** There are seven health problems in the puzzle. Find the other six.
Look in these directions (↓ →).

A	T	O	O	T	H	A	C	H	E	W	A
B	C	K	F	M	U	U	O	E	R	F	L
S	O	R	E	T	H	R	O	A	T	D	L
R	U	I	V	D	E	I	H	D	U	J	E
V	G	J	P	L	A	R	U	P	L	A	F
E	H	C	S	H	E	A	D	A	C	H	E
S	I	O	T	B	J	W	L	S	A	N	V
O	H	L	F	O	V	A	O	U	B	D	E
B	E	A	L	L	E	R	G	I	E	S	R
G	A	N	G	D	C	K	S	W	N	C	H
S	T	O	M	A	C	H	A	C	H	E	I
R	M	R	L	T	N	F	R	G	C	S	R

B Look at the picture. Write sentences with the words from part A.

Joe   Taro   Chad   Amy   Jim and Liz   Sara   Joyce

1. _Joe has a fever._ 5. _____
2. _____ 6. _____
3. _____ 7. _____
4. _____

2 I feel sick.

Grammar and vocabulary

Look at the pictures. Write questions and answers.

Ann / the flu

Dan / a cold

1. What does Ann do when she has the flu?
   When Ann has the flu, she stays in bed.

2. _____
   If _____

Rick / a headache

Pat / a toothache

3. _____
   _____ when _____

4. _____
   _____ if _____

3 About you

Grammar and vocabulary

Write questions for a friend using *when* or *if*. Then answer your friend's questions.

1. *You* What do you do when you're sick?
   (when / are sick)

   Friend When I'm sick, I stay home and watch movies all day. How about you?

   You _____

2. *You* _____
   (if / have a bad cough)

   Friend I chat on the Internet instead of on the phone if I have a bad cough. And you?

   You _____

3. *You* _____
   (if / get a stomachache)

   Friend If I get a stomachache, I drink water. I don't eat a lot. How about you?

   You _____

4. *You* _____
   (when / have a fever)

   Friend When I have a fever, I take aspirin. I don't go out. What about you?

   You _____

How come you're tired?

1 *It's my allergies.*

Conversation strategies **Complete the conversation. Use the sentences in the box.**

> Headaches too? Do you take anything? ✓ Oh, no! Do you sneeze a lot?
>
> You're kidding! How come? Gosh, that's terrible! So, what are you studying?
>
> Are you serious? You can't study? Really? But how can you study when you feel sick?

Joan What's the matter, Gary? Your nose and eyes are red.

Gary Oh, it's my allergies. I always feel this way in the spring.

Joan Oh, no! Do you sneeze a lot?

Gary Oh, yes. I sneeze all the time. And I get headaches.

Joan _____

Gary Not really. Actually, I don't like to take medicine.

Joan _____

Gary Well, if I take medicine, I can't study.

Joan _____

Gary Well, you see, when I take medicine, I always fall asleep.

Joan _____

Gary It's hard, but I need to. I have a big test next week.

Joan _____

Gary I'm studying to be a doctor.

2 *You're kidding!*

Conversation strategies **Circle the best response to show surprise.**

1. My wife talks in her sleep.
   a. My wife does too.
   b. Wow! What does she say?

2. I love getting up early on weekends.
   a. I always get up early.
   b. Early? I like to sleep late.

3. I take two or three naps every day.
   a. Oh! Are you sleeping enough at night?
   b. I know. And you snore, too.

4. I eat a lot of chocolate when I can't sleep.
   a. Me too. I love to eat chocolate at night.
   b. You're kidding! I can't sleep when I eat chocolate.

5. My grandfather goes running six days a week.
   a. No way! How old is he?
   b. I see. He's very healthy, right?

6. I often dream about food.
   a. I do too. I always dream about ice cream.
   b. Food? Are you hungry when you go to bed?

7. I have three part-time jobs.
   a. It's important to work hard.
   b. Really? Aren't you tired a lot?

8. If I can't sleep, I always listen to rock or hip-hop.
   a. Me too. I also listen to pop music.
   b. Gosh! Why not classical or jazz?

3 No way!

Write responses to show surprise. Then ask follow-up questions.

1. *A* My friends Chuck and Tina exercise when they can't sleep.

   B _No way!_   _What kind of exercise do they do?_

2. *A* My best friend never remembers her dreams.

   B _____   _____

3. *A* I sometimes sleep at the office.

   B _____   _____

4. *A* Sometimes I can't sleep because my dog snores.

   B _____   _____

5. *A* My brother has the same nightmare once a week.

   B _____   _____

6. *A* My father sleepwalks every night.

   B _____   _____

7. *A* I never use an alarm clock.

   B _____   _____

8. *A* My brother goes running right after he eats dinner.

   B _____   _____

4 About you

Answer the questions with your own information.

1. Are you feeling sleepy right now? _____

2. How often do you take naps on weekdays? _____

3. Do you ever sleep in class or at work? _____

4. Are you sleeping well these days? _____

5. What do you do when you wake up at night? _____

6. Do you dream in color? _____

Ways to relax

1 The practice of yoga

Reading **A Read the article. Find the answers to these questions.**

1. Where does yoga come from? _____
2. Is yoga good for stress? _____
3. Can you practice yoga alone? _____
4. Do children do yoga, too? _____

East Meets West

The ancient Eastern art of yoga is more than 5,000 years old. It's a combination of relaxation, stretching, breathing, a vegetarian diet, positive thinking, and meditation.

Yoga originated in India, but today it is becoming more and more popular in the United States. Why do Americans do yoga? One survey of yoga enthusiasts found out.

A majority (55%) of the people in the survey practice yoga because they want to relax. Some people do yoga to stay in shape. And other people do yoga when they feel depressed, have headaches, or have a lot of stress. Yoga is also helpful for people who have trouble sleeping.

What do people do when they practice yoga? Most of the people in the survey (90%) practice poses and breathing exercises. Half of them also meditate.

Where do Americans do yoga? Many people in the survey (48%) take classes at a local yoga studio. Others (39%) do it at home, either alone or with friends. A few people (9%) have a private teacher.

And how long do people do yoga? Most people in the survey (57%) do it for half an hour or an hour at a time. Some (41%) do yoga for an hour and a half. They all say it doesn't matter how often you do it – it's just important to do it. And it seems everyone is doing it these days. It's even popular with children!

Yoga keeps people healthy because it makes them strong and helps them relax, sleep, and cope with stress. So what about you? Would you like to try yoga?

B Read the article again. Then answer the questions.

1. What kind of diet do yoga teachers recommend? _a vegetarian diet_____
2. Why do Americans do yoga? Give three reasons. _____
3. What percentage of people in the survey practice poses and breathing? _____
4. Do most Americans in the survey do yoga at home? _____
5. According to the article, how long do most people do yoga? _____
6. Would you like to try yoga? Why or why not? _____

24

2 Healthy lifestyles

A Read these suggestions for a healthy lifestyle. Put in commas where necessary.

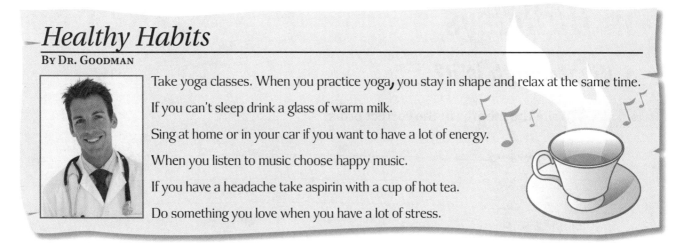

Healthy Habits
BY DR. GOODMAN

Take yoga classes. When you practice yoga, you stay in shape and relax at the same time.

If you can't sleep drink a glass of warm milk.

Sing at home or in your car if you want to have a lot of energy.

When you listen to music choose happy music.

If you have a headache take aspirin with a cup of hot tea.

Do something you love when you have a lot of stress.

B Choose a title and write a short article. Give three suggestions.

Sleep	Food and Diet	Exercise

Unit 3 Progress chart

Mark the boxes below to rate your progress. ☑ = I know how to . . . ? = I need to review how to . . .	To review, go back to these pages in the Student's Book.
Grammar ☐ make statements with the simple present and present continuous	22 and 23
☐ ask questions with the simple present and present continuous	22 and 23
☐ use *if* and *when* in statements and questions	25
Vocabulary ☐ name at least 8 healthy habits	22 and 23
☐ name at least 4 unhealthy habits	22 and 23
☐ name at least 6 health problems	24 and 25
Conversation strategies ☐ keep a conversation going with comments and follow-up questions	26 and 27
☐ use expressions like *Wow!* or *You're kidding!* to show surprise	27
Writing ☐ use commas in *if* and *when* clauses	29

Unit 4 Celebrations

Birthdays

1 What month is it?

 A Write the months in the correct order.

_____ January _____   _____ _____   _____ _____
_____ _____   _____ _____   _____ _____
_____ _____   _____ _____   _____ _____

B Complete the sentences with the correct numbers.

1. January is the ___first___ month of the year.
2. March is the _____ month of the year.
3. June is the _____ month of the year.
4. July is the _____ month of the year.
5. October is the _____ month of the year.
6. December is the _____ month of the year.

2 When's her birthday?

Grammar and vocabulary

Look at the dates. Then write each person's birthday two ways.

1. Halle Berry's birthday is on August fourteenth.
   Halle Berry's birthday is on the fourteenth of August.

2. _____
   _____

3. _____
   _____

4. _____
   _____

5. _____
   _____

6. _____
   _____

① Halle Berry 8/14
② Jackie Chan 4/7
③ Jude Law 12/29
④ Drew Barrymore 2/22
⑤ Sofia Coppola 5/14
⑥ Ronaldo 9/22

3 Future plans

Grammar **Complete the conversations with the correct form of *going to*.**

1. **Sam** What <u>are you going to do</u> (you / do) this weekend?

   Diane I _____ (see) my grandmother. We _____ (have) a birthday party for her.

   Sam That's nice. So, _____ (it / be) a big party?

   Diane No, not really. We _____ (not do) much. It _____ (be) just the family. Mom _____ (bake) her a cake. Then her friends _____ (take) her dancing. She's a tango teacher.

   Sam Your grandmother's a tango teacher? Cool.

2. **Yumi** That was Jun on the phone. He can't take us to Sarah's party.

   Kara Oh, no. Why not?

   Yumi No car. His parents are going to the mountains, and they _____ (take) the car.

   Kara Well, we can't drive. Who else _____ (be) there?

   Yumi Dan, but he _____ (not go) until after work.

   Kara Well, it looks like we _____ (walk). Wear comfortable shoes!

4 Happy birthday!

Grammar and vocabulary **Complete the card with the correct pronouns.**

Dear Kathleen,

Happy birthday! I'm sending ___you___ (you / her) this card from Mexico. Hector and I are in Mexico City visiting his parents. His parents are showing _____ (them / us) all the sights. His mother is so nice. I brought _____ (her / him) some jewelry from New York, and she wears it everywhere.

His mother is teaching _____ (you / me) how to make Mexican food. She's going to send _____ (them / us) a tamale pot when we get home. Hector loves tamales, so I can make _____ (him / her) tamales next Christmas. We want to do something special for his parents, but we can't give _____ (us / them) anything because they won't let us!

How about you? Can I bring _____ (you / me) anything from Mexico for your birthday?

Ellen

Special days

1 Good times

Vocabulary Look at the pictures. Write the special event. Then complete the descriptions with the expressions in the box.

blow out the candle	go out for a romantic dinner	shout "Happy New Year"
exchange rings	go trick-or-treating	✓ sing "Happy Birthday"
get a diploma	have a reception	✓ wear a cap and gown
give her chocolates	see fireworks	wear costumes

graduation day

birthday

1. Ana and her classmates are going to <u>wear a cap and gown</u>. When they call her name, Ana's going to _____ .

2. The waiters are going to <u>sing "Happy Birthday"</u> and bring Erin a cake. She's going to make a wish and _____ .

3. Allen and Carine are going to _____ . After dinner, Allen's going to _____ .

4. Bruce and Sheila are going to a big party. They're going to _____ on the beach. Then at midnight, they're going to _____ .

5. Ahmad and Keisha are going to get married. During the wedding, they're going to _____ . After the wedding, they're going to _____ .

6. John and Rudy are going to _____ of their favorite comic-book characters. When they're ready, they're going to _____ in the neighborhood.

2 A busy week

Grammar Read George's calendar. Write a sentence about each plan. Use the present continuous.

May

Sunday	Monday	Tuesday	Wednesday	Thursday	Friday	Saturday
8 Mother's Day - Have lunch with Mom.	9 **8:00** - Meet Ann for dinner.	10 Tennis after work	11 Lunch with Joe	12 Yoga before work	13 **2:00** - Go to Keith and Karen's wedding.	14 **5:00** - Go to Jennifer's graduation party.

1. On May eighth, George is having lunch with his mother.
2. _____
3. _____
4. _____
5. _____
6. _____
7. _____

3 What's going to happen?

Grammar Write a prediction about each picture. Use *going to* or *not going to*.

1. It's not going to be sunny.
    (sunny)
2. _____
    (trick-or-treating)
3. _____
    (flowers)

4. _____
    (fireworks)
5. _____
    (diploma)
6. _____
    (snow)

1 "Vague" expressions

Conversation strategies **Complete the conversations. Use** *and everything* **or** *and things (like that)*. **Leave two blanks empty in each conversation.**

1. *Maya* What are you doing on New Year's?

   Brittany Well, my family's having dinner at my grandmother's house _____ . You know, a big dinner with ham and mashed potatoes ___and everything___ .

   Maya Sounds great! Do you have pies _____ ?

   Brittany Yeah, but I'm trying to lose weight. There's all this holiday food like cookies _____ . It's really hard to be on a diet.

   Maya Yeah, I have the same problem. And I work at a bakery _____ . So let's enjoy the holidays and diet next year.

   Brittany Great idea! I'm hungry. Let's go out and eat some cake, ice cream, _____ .

2. *Carol* Can we do something romantic for our anniversary this year _____ ? Can you give me chocolates, send me flowers, _____ ?

   Bill Sure, I can do that _____ .

   Carol And I'd like to go out for a nice dinner.

   Bill Well, it depends. Where do you want to go?

   Carol Somewhere with violin music and candles _____ .

   Bill OK. . . . Uh, do you want a present, too?

   Carol Of course! I'd like some jewelry, some clothes, _____ .

   Bill Oh. When's our anniversary again?

   Carol On the twenty-fifth.

   Bill Well, I need to get a weekend job to pay for all this.

3. *Sonia* Hey, the Rodeo Days festival starts tomorrow _____ . So, what is it exactly?

   Pete Well, every February, kids dress up in cowboy costumes. They wear hats and ride horses, and there's a parade _____ . Are you going?

   Sonia Maybe. I don't know, I'm not big on cowboys _____ .

   Pete Well, it's really kind of fun. And people are going to sell jewelry and T-shirts _____ .

   Sonia I can go shopping there? Wow, I'm going to have a lot of fun at this festival _____ .

2 About you

Answer the questions with the responses in the box. Use each response only once. Then add more information or a follow-up question.

| It depends. | Maybe. | ✓I don't know. | I'm not sure. |

1. Are you going to celebrate your birthday with a party and everything?

   <u>I don't know. My girlfriend usually surprises me on my birthday.</u>

2. What do you want to do this weekend?

   _____

3. Are you going to send your mom some flowers on her birthday?

   _____

4. Do you want to go see the fireworks tonight?

   _____

3 Scrambled conversation

Number the lines of the conversation in the correct order.

[ ] But you can also shop for cool Chinese gifts and things.

[1] Would you like to go to a Chinese festival?

[ ] OK. So, what do people do?

[ ] There's going to be free food? Great, I'd love to go.

[ ] Well, I don't know. I'm not big on dances and stuff like that.

[ ] Well, at least the food is great, and it's free.

[ ] Uh, maybe, but I don't have money for shopping right now.

[ ] It's for Chinese New Year.

[ ] Lots of things, like lion dances and everything!

[ ] I'm not sure. What kind of festival is it exactly?

1 Celebrating mothers

Reading **A** Read the article. Then add the correct heading to each paragraph.

| Traditional ways to celebrate | History of the holiday | When is Mother's Day? |
| Ideas for Mother's Day | ✓ Why people celebrate Mother's Day | |

Mother's Day

Why people celebrate Mother's Day

In many countries, there is a special day of the year when children of all ages celebrate their mothers. On this day – Mother's Day – children tell their mothers that they love them, and thank them for their love and care.

Mother's Day is not a new celebration. Historians say that it started as a spring festival in ancient Greece. The modern festival of Mother's Day probably comes from England in the 1600s, when people had a day off from their jobs to visit their mothers on a day they called "Mothering Sunday." They took small gifts and a special cake called "simnel cake." In the United States, Mother's Day became an official holiday in 1914.

People in different countries celebrate Mother's Day on different days. In Australia, Brazil, Italy, Japan, Turkey, and the United States, it's on the second Sunday in May, whereas in France and Sweden, it's on the last Sunday in May. In Argentina, Mother's Day is celebrated on the second Sunday in October, whereas in Spain and Portugal, it's on December 8.

Although many countries celebrate Mother's Day at different times of the year, the holidays have one purpose in common – to show love and appreciation for mothers. For example, on Mother's Day morning, some children bring their mothers breakfast in bed. Others give their mothers gifts they made especially for this holiday. And adults buy their mothers flowers or send them cards.

What are you going to do next Mother's Day? Maybe you can use some of these ideas to make your mother feel special.

- *make or buy your mother a beautiful Mother's Day card*
- *write her a letter telling her why you appreciate her*
- *do a special chore for her*
- *make her a special meal or bake a cake*
- *buy her some flowers or her favorite candy*
- *plant a flower or tree somewhere she can see it*

B Read the article again. Answer the questions.

1. Where did the idea of Mother's Day come from originally? _____

2. Which country started the tradition of giving presents on Mother's Day? _____

3. What was Mother's Day called in England? _____

4. When do Brazil and Japan celebrate Mother's Day? _____

5. What are three traditions on Mother's Day? _____

_____

2 Making plans

Writing **A** Start and end these notes to different people.

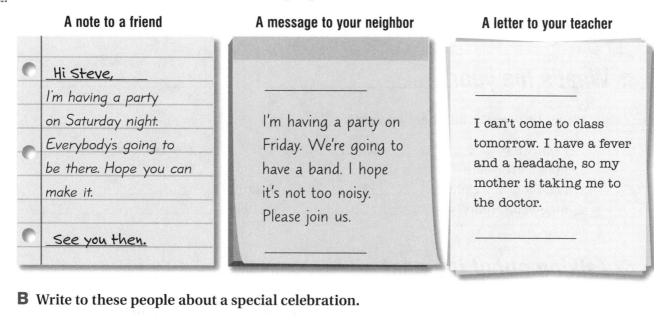

A note to a friend

Hi Steve,
I'm having a party
on Saturday night.
Everybody's going to
be there. Hope you can
make it.

See you then.

A message to your neighbor

_____

I'm having a party on
Friday. We're going to
have a band. I hope
it's not too noisy.
Please join us.

_____

A letter to your teacher

_____

I can't come to class
tomorrow. I have a fever
and a headache, so my
mother is taking me to
the doctor.

_____

B Write to these people about a special celebration.

A note to a teacher

A message to a friend

A letter to your grandparents

Unit 4 Progress chart

Mark the boxes below to rate your progress. ☑ = I know how to . . . ? = I need to review how to . . .	To review, go back to these pages in the Student's Book.
Grammar	
☐ use *going to* for the future	35, 36, and 37
☐ use indirect objects and indirect object pronouns	34 and 35
☐ use the present continuous for specific future plans	37
Vocabulary	
☐ name the months of the year	34 and 35
☐ name the days of the month (ordinal numbers 1–31)	34 and 35
Conversation strategies	
☐ use "vague" expressions like *and everything* and *and things*	38 and 39
☐ use "vague" responses like *Maybe* and *It depends*	39
Writing	
☐ start and end invitations and personal notes	41

Unit 5 Growing up

Childhood

1 What's the year?

Vocabulary Write the years in numbers or words.

1. twenty ten _____2010_____
2. nineteen oh-four _____
3. two thousand eight _____
4. nineteen seventy-seven _____
5. 1982 _____nineteen eighty-two_____
6. 2006 _____
7. 2013 _____
8. 1998 _____

2 Talking about the past

Grammar Complete the conversations with *was, wasn't, were, weren't, did,* or *didn't.*

1. **Rick** So, Dina, ___did___ you grow up here in Miami?

   Dina Yes, I _____ , but we _____ born here.
   My sister and I _____ born in Puerto Rico,
   and we moved here when we _____ kids.

   Rick _____ you study English when you _____
   in school in Puerto Rico?

   Dina Yes, we _____ – for a few years – but we _____
   really learn English until we came here.

   Rick Wow! And now you speak English better
   than I do – and I _____ born here!

2. **Thomas** When ___were___ you born, Grandma?

   Grandma I _____ born in 1929.

   Thomas Really? _____ you born here in Los Angeles?

   Grandma No, I _____ . Your grandfather and I _____
   both born in China.

   Thomas So when _____ you come to the U.S.?

   Grandma My family _____ move here until I _____
   13 years old.

   Thomas _____ you go to school in China?

   Grandma No, I _____ . My parents _____ rich,
   so I had to work.

   Thomas And when _____ Grandpa born?

   Grandma He _____ born in 1928, but he says
   he _____ really born until 1947.

   Thomas Why does he say that?

   Grandma Because that's when he met *me.*

3 A life story

Grammar

Complete the story with the words in the box. You can use some words more than once.

✓ago	for	from	in	last	long	then	to	until	when

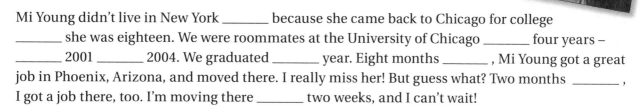

This is a picture of my best friend, Mi Young. I took it a few years __ago__ .
Mi Young and I met _____ 1988. We were very young _____ we became
friends. Mi Young is a very interesting person. She was born in Busan, South
Korea, _____ 1984. Her family moved to the U.S. _____ she was three
years old. They lived in Chicago _____ Mi Young was fifteen. _____ they
moved to New York City. I cried _____ a long time after they moved.

Mi Young didn't live in New York _____ because she came back to Chicago for college
_____ she was eighteen. We were roommates at the University of Chicago _____ four years –
_____ 2001 _____ 2004. We graduated _____ year. Eight months _____ , Mi Young got a great
job in Phoenix, Arizona, and moved there. I really miss her! But guess what? Two months _____ ,
I got a job there, too. I'm moving there _____ two weeks, and I can't wait!

4 About you

Grammar and vocabulary

Unscramble the questions. Then answer the questions with your own information.

1. you / When / born / were ? _When were you born?_ _____

   _____

2. Where / born / your / were / parents ? _____

   _____

3. grow up / you / Where / did ? _____

   _____

4. best friend / Who / your / was / ago / five years ? _____

   _____

5. a child / you / move / when / Did / ever / were / you ? _____

   _____

6. you / play video games / Did / when / you / little / were ? _____

   _____

7. long / you / were / elementary school / How / in ? _____

   _____

1 What's the subject?

Vocabulary **A** **Circle the word that doesn't belong. Then write the general category of the subjects.**

1. history   (chemistry)   economics   geography   _social studies_
2. gymnastics   dance   art   track   _____
3. geometry   computer studies   algebra   calculus   _____
4. literature   biology   chemistry   physics   _____
5. choir   band   drama   orchestra   _____

B **Complete the crossword puzzle.**

Across

1. In this math subject, you see the letters *x* and *y* a lot.
7. I can run fast and jump high. I'm good at this P.E. subject.
8. Students sing in this music class.
9. In this subject, you study about people and things from a long time ago.
10. Students learn to be actors when they study this subject.

Down

2. In this class, you study the countries of the world and their oceans, rivers, and mountains.
3. You draw and paint in this class.
4. This subject is a science. You learn about plant and animal life.
5. In this subject, teachers ask students to read novels, stories, and poems.
6. In this class, students play classical music on instruments.

Crossword grid:
1. a l 2.g e b r 3.a
(with numbered cells 4., 5., 6., 7., 8., 9., 10.)

2 *How did we do?*

Grammar   **A** Write the determiners in order in the chart below.

| a few | ✓all | a lot of | most | none | some |

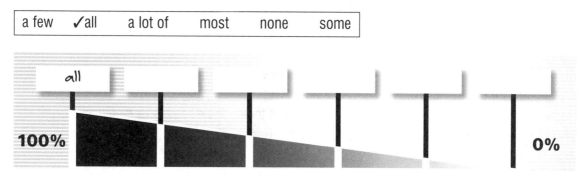

all

100%   0%

B Read the test results. Complete the sentences with the determiners in the box. Use each expression only once.

	Chemistry	English	Geography	Geometry
Passed	55%	100%	90%	15%
Failed	45%	0%	10%	85%

| A few | A few of | All of | A lot of | Most of | None of | ✓Some | Some of |

1. ____Some____ students in the class passed chemistry. _____ them failed chemistry.

2. _____ the students passed English. _____ the students failed it.

3. _____ the students passed geography. _____ students failed it.

4. _____ the students passed geometry. _____ people failed it.

3 *About you*

Grammar and vocabulary   Answer the questions. Write true sentences using determiners.

When you were in high school, what was a subject . . .

1. most of your friends liked? _Most of my friends liked P.E._

2. all of the students had to study? _____

3. a lot of students hated? _____

4. some of your classmates loved? _____

5. no students ever failed? _____

6. a few students were always really good at? _____

7. none of your classmates liked? _____

8. a lot of students got good grades in? _____

9. some students dropped? _____

Well, actually, . . .

1 Correcting things you say

Complete the conversations with the sentences in the box.

Actually, no, it was 2002.   Well, no, I guess I spent some weekends with my grandparents.
Well, at least most of them didn't.   Well, not perfect, actually. My dad lost his job.
No, wait. I was nine.   ✓Well, not all of them. Josie speaks three languages.
Well, actually, it was dark brown.   No, wait. . . . Her name was Mrs. Santos.
Actually, no, I was 18 when I quit.

1. *A* All my friends are bilingual. They all speak two languages.

   Well, not all of them. Josie speaks three languages.

   B That's amazing!

2. *A* My best friend and I had sleepovers every weekend when we were kids.

   _____

   B That sounds like fun.

3. *A* We moved to Rio de Janeiro when I was ten.

   _____

   B So you were pretty young.

4. *A* I was on a swimming team until I was 16.

   _____

   B That's the reason you swim so well.

5. *A* My brother and I had a perfect childhood.

   _____

   B Really? But you were generally pretty happy, right?

6. *A* My cousin lived with us for a year – in 2003, I think.

   _____

   B That was your cousin Alice, right?

7. *A* My favorite teacher in elementary school was Mrs. Santana.

   _____

   B Oh, yeah? My favorite teacher was Mr. Stiller.

8. *A* When I was little, none of my friends had pets.

   _____

   B But you had a dog, right?

9. *A* I had black hair when I was born.

   _____

   B Really? I was born with no hair at all!

2 I mean

Complete the questions using *I mean* to correct the underlined words. Then answer the questions.

1. When you were a child, what was the name of your first <u>professor</u>, _I mean, teacher_ ?

   _____

2. Were you six or seven when you started <u>high school</u>, _____?

   _____

3. In elementary school, did you have lunch in the school <u>café</u>, _____?

   _____

4. As a kid, what was your favorite <u>sport</u>, _____?

   Did you like checkers? _____

5. When you were young, did you play any <u>music</u>, _____, like the piano?

   _____

3 About you

Complete these sentences so they are true for you.

1. I started school when I was three. Actually, no,

   _when I was five_____ .

2. The name of my elementary school was Park Elementary.

   No, wait. . . . _____ .

3. My first teacher's name was Miss Parker, I mean,

   _____ .

4. I always got good grades in every subject.

   Well, _____ .

5. Most of my childhood friends liked classical music.

   Well, no, _____ .

6. When I was a child, my favorite holiday was Halloween,

   I mean, _____ .

7. I remember all my classmates in kindergarten.

   Well, actually, _____ .

8. A lot of my friends did gymnastics after school.

   No, wait. . . . _____ .

Teenage years

1 Small-town story

Reading **A** Read the story of Yolanda's life. Then number the pictures in the correct order.

INTERVIEW: *A happy childhood* by *Kathy Montaño*

Kathy Montaño grew up in the small town of Bagdad, Arizona. She interviewed several Mexican Americans in Bagdad about their childhood. This is the story of Yolanda Sandoval.

"My name is Yolanda Sandoval. I was born in Cananea, Mexico, on June 13, 1922. My parents brought me to Bagdad when I was six months old. My father's name was Francisco Sandoval, and my mother's name was Cecilia Bernal.

I was their first child. I have four younger brothers. My mother gave Rafael, my third brother, her name as a middle name. Apart from Rafael, no one had a middle name. My mother was very gentle and patient. She died when I was 16. My father was very kind but strict.

What did my father do for a living? He worked in a mine. He didn't talk much about his work, maybe because he didn't like it. My mother didn't go to work. She stayed home to take care of us.

My mother always did special things for our birthdays. One year she gave me a purple party. Everything was purple, even the drinks! She also made me a purple dress. That was the best party I ever had. I invited all my friends – except for Bobby. I was angry with him at the time.

My brothers and I loved the movies. We thought they were wonderful. A man named Angel Ruiz always showed old cowboy movies at the local theater, and we went to all of them. He charged five cents for a movie. Sometimes we didn't have the five cents, but he let us see the movie anyway.

What about school? What subjects did I study? I had to study English for four years, science for two (I took chemistry and biology), and a foreign language for two years. I took Spanish, of course! Spanish was easy for me, so I got good grades. I also studied U.S. history, home economics, and physical education. I loved school!"

B Read Yolanda's story again. Then complete the sentences.

1. Kathy Montaño interviewed several people in her town about _____ .

2. Yolanda Sandoval came to Bagdad when she _____ .

3. Yolanda's father didn't talk much about his work because _____ .

4. On Yolanda's birthday one year, her mother gave her _____ .

5. At the local movie theater, Yolanda and her brothers saw _____ .

6. Yolanda studied English for _____ .

2 When I was a teenager

A Answer these questions about your first year in high school. Use *except (for)* or *apart from*.

1. Did you like your teachers?

   I liked all my teachers except for my history teacher, Mr. Crown.

2. Did you get along with your parents?

   _____

3. Did you enjoy your high school subjects?

   _____

4. Did you get along with all your classmates?

   _____

5. Did you and your best friend do a lot of things together?

   _____

B Write about some of your favorite activities when you were a teenager.

When I was a teenager, I lived in

My friends and I loved to

Unit 5 Progress chart

Mark the boxes below to rate your progress. ☑ = I know how to . . . ? = I need to review how to . . .	To review, go back to these pages in the Student's Book.
Grammar	
☐ make statements and ask questions with the simple past and past of *be*	44 and 45
☐ talk about the past using time expressions	44 and 45
☐ use determiners: *all (of), most (of), a lot of, some (of), a few (of), no, none of*	46 and 47
Vocabulary	
☐ say years	44 and 45
☐ name at least 12 school subjects	47
☐ name at least 5 general subject categories	47
Conversation strategies	
☐ correct things I say with expressions like *Actually* and *No, wait*	48 and 49
☐ use *I mean* to correct myself	49
Writing	
☐ use *except (for)* and *apart from* to link ideas	51

Lesson A Out shopping

1 Where . . . ?

> Grammar and vocabulary

Look at the map. Write two answers for each question.

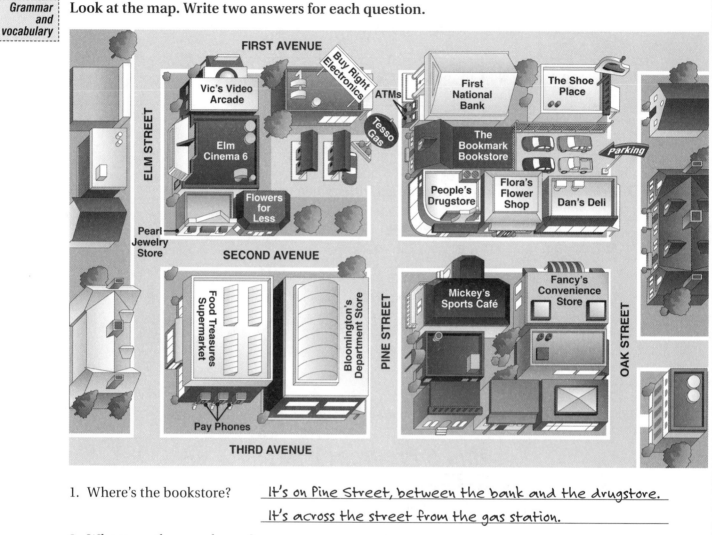

1. Where's the bookstore?   <u>It's on Pine Street, between the bank and the drugstore.</u>
   <u>It's across the street from the gas station.</u>

2. Where are the pay phones? _____
   _____

3. Where's the parking lot? _____
   _____

4. Where are the ATMs? _____
   _____

5. Where's the gas station? _____
   _____

6. Where's the drugstore? _____
   _____

2 *Looking for places*

Grammar

Write questions. Then complete the answers with *there's one, there are some, there isn't one,* **or** *there aren't any.*

1. *A* <u>Is there a drugstore around here?</u> (drugstore / around here ?)

   B Yes, <u>there's one</u> on the corner of Pine Street and Second Avenue.

2. *A* _____ (parking lot / near here ?)

   B _____ on Oak Street, behind the bookstore.

3. *A* _____ (video arcades / anywhere ?)

   B _____ over there, next to the electronics store.

4. *A* _____ (museum / in this town ?)

   B No, sorry, _____ .

5. *A* _____ (public restrooms / near here ?)

   B No, _____ public restrooms near here, but there are some

   inside the department store on Pine Street.

6. *A* _____ (pay phones / around here ?)

   B Yeah, sure, _____ on Third Avenue.

3 *About you*

Grammar and vocabulary

Write questions. Then answer the questions about your neighborhood.

1. *A* (a good coffee shop) <u>Is there a good coffee shop in this neighborhood?</u>

   B <u>Yes, there is. There's Emily's on the corner of Center Avenue and First Street.</u>

2. *A* (a big department store) _____

   B _____

3. *A* (any Internet cafés) _____

   B _____

4. *A* (a convenience store) _____

   B _____

5. *A* (any cheap restaurants) _____

   B _____

Getting around

1 Places in town

Vocabulary   Complete the sentences with the places in the box.

✓aquarium	museum	running path	stadium	visitors' center
hotel	parking garage	skateboard ramp	theater	water park

You can . . .

1. see sea animals at an __aquarium__ .
2. swim in an outdoor pool at a _____ .
3. go jogging on a _____ .
4. go skateboarding on a _____ .
5. see a play at a _____ .

6. see art and interesting old things at a _____ .
7. ask for information at a _____ .
8. leave your car at a _____ .
9. watch a baseball game at a _____ .
10. sleep at a _____ .

2 Where am I going?

Vocabulary   Some people are at the Sea View Hotel. Where do they want to go? Look at the map. Complete the conversations with the names of the places.

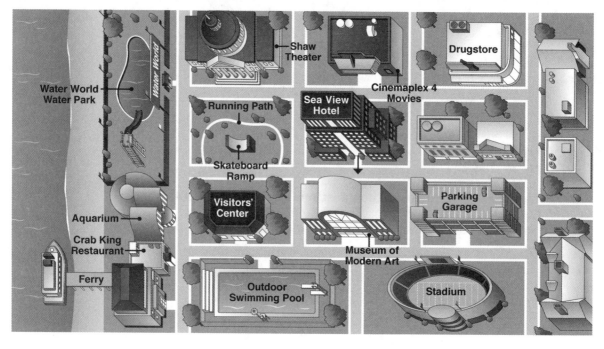

1. *A* Can you tell me how to get to the _____ ?
   B Sure. When you leave the hotel, turn right. It's on the next block. It's there on your right.

2. *A* Can you tell me how to get to the _____ ?
   B Yes. Go out of the hotel, and turn left. Turn left again at the corner, go one block, and turn right. It's on your left.

3. *A* Can you help me? I'd like to go to the _____ .
   B Yes. Turn right out of the hotel. Go straight for another block, and make a left. Walk two blocks. It's on your right, next to the restaurant.

3 Directions, directions

Rewrite the sentences to make requests. Then look at the map on page 44, and write directions.

1. You're at the Visitors' Center. "Tell me how to get to the museum."(Could)

   A _Could you tell me how to get to the museum?_

   B _Turn left. Walk straight ahead for a block._

   The museum is going to be right there on the left.

2. You're at the museum. "Give me directions to the aquarium." (Could)

   A _____

   B _____

3. You're at the aquarium. "Tell me how to get to the pool." (Can)

   A _____

   B _____

4. You're at the pool. "Recommend a good place for skateboarding." (Can)

   A _____

   B _____

5. You're at the skateboard ramp. "Give me directions to the Visitors' Center." (Can)

   A _____

   B _____

4 Can you help me?

Write requests and offers.

1. Make an offer: Ask how you can help the person.

   How can I help you?

2. Make a request: Ask for directions to the aquarium.

   _____

3. Make a request: Ask for help.

   _____

4. Make an offer: Ask someone what you can do.

   _____

5. Make a request: Ask someone to recommend a good place to go running.

   _____

Excuse me?

1 Checking information

Conversation strategies

Complete the conversations. Check the information.

1. *A* Hi. Where to?

   B I'm going to 830 Center Street.

   A <u>I'm sorry? Did you say 813 Center</u>
   <u>Street?</u>

   B No, 830. That's on the corner of Center and Main – on the left side of the street.

   A _____

   B Yes, the left side.

2. *A* Could you tell me how to get to Atlantic Bank?

   B _____

   A Yes. Do you know it?

   B I think so. Go straight ahead for three blocks, and turn left. The bank is on the right.

   A _____

   B No. Turn left. The bank is on the right.

3. *A* Can I help you?

   B Yes, please. What time does the next show start?

   A At 7:15.

   B _____

   A 7:15.

   B And what time does it end?

   A It ends at 9:05.

   B _____

   A Yes, that's right.

4. *A* Can you give me directions to a pet store?

   B _____

   A No, not a bookstore – a pet store. I want to buy some new fish for my aquarium.

   B Oh. Let me think. I think there's a pet store at Bay Street Mall.

   A _____

   B Bay Street Mall. It's about half an hour from here.

2 *Questions, questions*

Write an "echo" question for the underlined expression in each conversation.

1. *A* The concert tickets cost <u>sixty dollars each</u>.
   B <u>They cost how much?</u>

2. *A* There's a <u>great bicycle path</u> in the park.
   B _____

3. *A* The stadium is <u>on State Street</u>.
   B _____

4. *A* The aquarium closes at <u>8:30</u> on Friday nights.
   B _____

5. *A* Let's go to the museum. It's <u>just a few blocks away</u>.
   B _____

3 *I'm sorry?*

Complete the "echo" question in each conversation.

1. *A* A new deli opened right across the street from us.
   B I'm sorry, a new __what__ opened?
   A A new deli.
   B Great! Now I don't have to cook!

2. *A* Tim spent almost five hundred dollars on theater tickets for his family.
   B Excuse me? He spent _____ ?
   A Almost five hundred dollars.
   B Wow! I hope the play's good!

3. *A* I really want to leave at 6:00.
   B Sorry? You want to leave at _____ ?
   A At 6:00.
   B Uh-oh. We're late!

4. *A* Howard is going to the aquarium today.
   B I'm sorry? He's going _____ ?
   A To the aquarium. You know, the one on Main Street.
   B Oops! I told him I'd meet him there.

1 Life down under

A Look at the pictures. Check (✓) the items you think the article talks about.

☐ an amusement park
☐ an underground hotel
☐ a rock and roll museum

☐ a place that looks like the moon
☐ a drive-in movie theater
☐ an opal mine

B Read the article. How many of your guesses in part A are correct?

Coober Pedy

Coober Pedy – the Opal Capital of the World

Welcome to the desert town of Coober Pedy in the outback of Australia. The name Coober Pedy comes from the Aboriginal words *kupa piti*, which mean "white man in a hole." We hope you'll come visit.

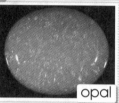
opal

Explorers first found opals in this area on February 1, 1915. In 1946, an Aboriginal woman named Tottie Bryant dug out a large and valuable opal. After that, a lot of people came to Coober Pedy to mine opals.

During the 1960s, many European immigrants came to work here, and Coober Pedy quickly became a large modern town. Today, Coober Pedy is the world's main source of high-quality opals and a unique tourist spot.

It's so hot in Coober Pedy that a lot of people live underground!

There are many underground homes, as well as underground hotels, museums, opal shops, art galleries, and, of course, opal mines.

We recommend that you visit these places when you come to Coober Pedy:

The Opal Mine & Museum is a unique underground museum about the history of the town. It includes a model underground home and a small opal mine. Some of the world's finest opals are on display here.

The Moon Plain is a large rocky area unlike anywhere else. It looks like the moon – or another planet! It was the set for many movies, including *Mad Max Beyond Thunderdome; The Adventures of Priscilla, Queen of the Desert*; and *The Red Planet*. It is about 15 kilometers northeast of Coober Pedy.

Coober Pedy Drive-In is an open-air movie theater. You can see four movies a month here – every other weekend on Friday and Saturday nights.

C Read the article on Coober Pedy again. Then match the two parts of each sentence.

1. The name Coober Pedy means __d__
2. Tottie Bryant found ____
3. Coober Pedy became a modern mining town when ____
4. At present, Coober Pedy is the world's main source ____
5. As a tourist place, Coober Pedy is famous for ____
6. The Moon Plain was ____

a. the set for many movies.
b. a very big and valuable opal.
c. its underground homes, museums, stores, and mines.
d. "white man in a hole."
e. immigrants came to work in the mines.
f. of high-quality opals.

2 Walking guide

A Read this New Orleans walking tour. Look at the map, and fill in the missing words.

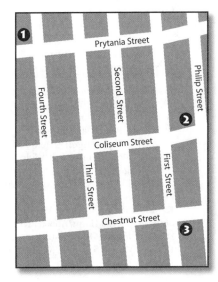

Start at #1. This is the Garden District Book Shop. Anne Rice, a famous author from New Orleans, calls this her favorite bookstore.

Now go to #2. Take Prytania Street _four_ blocks to Philip Street. Turn _____ on Philip Street. Take Philip Street one _____ to Coliseum Street. _____ a right on Coliseum Street. They're on the _____ . These homes are called the Seven Sisters. A man wanted his seven daughters to live close to him. He built these seven houses for them as wedding gifts.

Now go to #3. Go _____ on Coliseum Street, and walk to the end of the block. _____ left on First Street. Go _____ for one block. It's right there, on the _____ . This is the Brevard-Mahat-Rice House, where Anne Rice lives and works.

B Think of two tourist attractions in your town or city. Write directions from one to the other.

Start at

Unit 6 Progress chart

Mark the boxes below to rate your progress. ☑ = I know how to . . . ? = I need to review how to . . .	To review, go back to these pages in the Student's Book.
Grammar	
☐ use *Is there?* and *Are there?* to ask about places in a town	54 and 55
☐ use *across from*, *behind*, *between*, etc., to describe location	55
☐ make offers and requests with *Can* and *Could*	56 and 57
Vocabulary	
☐ name at least 15 places in a city or town	54, 55, and 56
Conversation strategies	
☐ check information by repeating key words and using "checking" expressions	58 and 59
☐ ask "echo" questions to check information	59
Writing	
☐ write a guide giving directions	61

Illustration credits

Kenneth Batelman: 42, 44
Dominic Bugatto: 14, 34
Daniel Chen: 6
Matt Collins: 40
Chuck Gonzales: 19, 29

Violet Lemay: 16
Frank Montagna: 10, 22, 30
Marilena Perilli: 5
Greg White: 20, 47
Terry Wong: 2, 3, 28

Photography credits

4 (*clockwise from top left*) ©Creatas; ©Index Stock; ©Creatas; ©Yuri Kadobnov/AFP/Getty Images/Newscom; ©Pegaz/Alamy; ©Punchstock
11 ©Stuart Pearce/age fotostock
12 (*top row, left to right*) ©Henry Diltz/Corbis; ©AP/Wide World Photos; ©Brett Coomer/AP/Wide World Photos; ©Frank Micelotta/Getty Images; (*bottom row, left to right*) ©Jennifer Szymaszek/AP/Wide World Photos; ©Tim Mosenfelder/Corbis; ©Mark J. Terril/AP/Wide World Photos; ©Robert Cianflone/Getty Images
13 (*top*) ©Robert E. Klein/AP/Wide World Photos; (*both bottom photos*) ©Lionel Hahn/Abaca Press/Newscom
15 (*both photos*) ©Punchstock
18 (*top*) ©David Schmidt/Masterfile; (*bottom*) ©Getty Images
21 (*clockwise from top left*) ©Mary Kate Denny/PhotoEdit; ©Dana White/PhotoEdit; ©Punchstock; ©Jose Luis Pelaez Inc./Corbis
24 (*left*) ©Alamy; (*right*) ©Surgi Stock/Getty Images
25 ©Punchstock
26 (*clockwise from top left*) ©Roberto Pfeil/AP/Wide World Photos; ©Russ Einhorn/Newscom; ©Chris Weeks/AP/Wide World Photos; ©Enrico Liverani/AP/Wide World Photos; ©Rufus F. Folkks/Corbis; ©JoeTakano/OrionPress/INFGoff.com/Newscom
31 ©Keren Su/China Span/Alamy
35 ©Michael Newman/PhotoEdit
39 ©Michael Newman/PhotoEdit
46 (*both photos*) ©Getty Images
48 (*clockwise from top left*) ©Carolina Biological/Visuals Unlimited; ©Ross Barnett/Lonely Planet Images; ©Alessandro Gandolfi/Index Stock

Text credits

Notes

Notes

TOUCHSTONE

JANET GOKAY
MARCIA FISK ONG

SERIES AUTHORS

MICHAEL McCARTHY
JEANNE McCARTEN
HELEN SANDIFORD

2A

VIDEO ACTIVITY PAGES

CAMBRIDGE
UNIVERSITY PRESS

Contents

Introduction: To the Student

Character descriptions

Touchstone Video is a fun-filled, compelling situational comedy featuring a group of young people who are friends. David Parker is a reporter. His roommate is Alex Santos, a personal trainer. David's friend Gio Ferrari is a student visiting from Italy. Liz Martin is a singer and Web designer. She lives with Yoko Suzuki, a chef. Kim Davis is David's co-worker. She works in an office.

Through the daily encounters and activities of these characters, you have the opportunity to see and hear the language of the Student's Book vividly come to life in circumstances both familiar and entertaining.

This is David Parker.
He's a reporter.

This is Yoko Suzuki.
She's a chef.

This is Alex Santos.
He's a personal trainer.

This is Gio Ferrari.
He's a student.
He's from Italy.

This is Liz Martin.
She's a Web designer
and singer.

This is Kim Davis.
She's David's co-worker.

The Video

Welcome to the *Touchstone* Video. In this video you will get to know six people who are friends: David, Liz, Yoko, Alex, Kim, and Gio. You can read about them on page iv.

You will also hear them use the English that you are studying in the *Touchstone* Student's Books. Each of the four levels of the Video breaks down as follows:

Episode 1	Act 1	Student's Book units 1–3
	Act 2	
	Act 3	

Episode 2	Act 1	Student's Book units 4–6
	Act 2	
	Act 3	

Episode 3	Act 1	Student's Book units 7–9
	Act 2	
	Act 3	

Episode 4	Act 1	Student's Book units 10–12
	Act 2	
	Act 3	

Explanation of the DVD Menu

To play one Episode of the Video:
- On the Main Menu, select *Episode Menu*.
- On the Episode Menu, select the appropriate *Play Episode*.

To play one Act of the Video:
- On the Main Menu, select *Episode Menu*.
- On the Episode Menu, select *Act Menu*.
- On the Act Menu, select the appropriate *Play Act*.

To play the Video with subtitles:
- On the Main Menu, Episode Menu, or Act Menu, select *Subtitles*.
- On the Subtitles Menu, select *Subtitles on*. The DVD will then automatically take you back to the menu you were on before.

To cancel the subtitles:
- On the Main Menu, Episode Menu, or Act Menu, select *Subtitles*.
- On the Subtitles Menu, select *Subtitles off*. The DVD will then automatically take you back to the menu you were on before.

The Worksheets

For each Act there are *Before you watch*, *While you watch*, and *After you watch* worksheets.

For *While you watch* worksheets:
- Find **DVD** [0] on your worksheet.
- Input this number on the Video menu using your remote control. The DVD will then play only the segment of the Video you need to watch to complete the task.

We hope you enjoy the *Touchstone* Video!

Before you watch

A Write the words in the box under the correct hobby.

a board game	a cookbook	golf clubs	in-line skates
a painting	pots and pans	weights	

1. _____

_____

2. _____

3. _____

4. _____

5. _____

6. _____

B Match the questions with the answers. Then practice with a partner.

1. What's your favorite kind of music? _____
2. Can you paint? _____
3. Do you like cooking? _____
4. Do you play any sports? _____
5. Are you getting rid of these skates? _____

a. No, I can't. But I'd like to learn. I love art.
b. No, sports aren't really my thing.
c. I love jazz and country music!
d. Yes, I am. I don't use them anymore.
e. Yes, I do, but I'm not cooking a lot these days. I'm too busy.

While you watch

A Circle the correct answers.

DVD 1
VHS 00:05
—01:11

1. The friends are having a stoop sale _____ weekend.
   a. this   b. next
2. A stoop is the stairs _____ a building.
   a. in front of   b. behind
3. At a stoop sale, you sell _____ stuff.
   a. old   b. new
4. David says it's a great way to make _____ .
   a. friends   b. money
5. David is a _____ .
   a. salesman   b. reporter

DVD 2
VHS 01:11
—04:26

B What does everyone bring to the sale? Match the items to the people.
(Some people bring two or three items.)

a. board games	d. in-line skates	g. a painting
b. Web design books	e. weights	h. cookbooks
c. golf clubs	f. pots and pans	i. CDs

David   **Yoko**   **Liz**   **Alex**

_____*a*_____   _____

Now look at the items that the friends are selling. Complete the sentences with the correct names.

1. _____ is a singer and Web page designer.
2. _____ is a chef.
3. _____ is a personal trainer and likes to paint.

While you watch

DVD 3
VHS 00:05
−00:19

C Circle the correct answers.

1. Liz and Yoko live **across** / **down** the hall from David.
2. David is excited about the sale because **he wants to meet the neighbors** / **he's writing an article**.
3. David is selling his board games because he **has a lot** / **doesn't like them**.
4. Yoko is selling pots and pans because **they're old** / **she has enough**.
5. Liz is selling the books about Web page design because **they're old** / **she has enough**.
6. Liz is selling a lot of **jazz** / **country** CDs.
7. Alex is selling weights because he's **buying new ones** / **not using them**.
8. Alex **is** / **isn't** painting a lot these days.
9. Gio wants to **keep** / **get rid** of a lot of things.
10. Gio is studying **math** / **business**, so he can help with advertising and prices.

DVD 4
VHS 01:11
−04:29

D Circle the correct answers.

1. Gio loves board games. How does David feel about board games?
   a. He loves them, too.   b. He doesn't like them.
2. David can't skate. What about Gio?
   a. He can skate well.   b. He can't skate, either.
3. What does Yoko think of golf?
   a. She likes it.   b. She doesn't like it.
4. How does David feel about golf?
   a. He likes it, too.   b. He doesn't like it, either.
5. How does Alex feel about golf?
   a. He loves it.   b. He doesn't like it very much.
6. What do Yoko and Liz think of Alex's painting?
   a. They like it.   b. They don't like it.
7. What does Gio think of the painting?
   a. He likes it, too.   b. He doesn't like it very much.

After you watch

A What can you remember? Who wants to sell each item? Who says they like each item?

1. the in-line skates   David wants to sell the skates.
2. the golf clubs   _____
3. Alex's painting   _____
4. the board games   _____

B Complete questions 6 and 7 with your own ideas. Answer the questions in the *You* column. Then ask a partner the questions.

	You	*Your partner*
1. Can you paint?	Yes / No	Yes / No
2. Can you play golf?	Yes / No	Yes / No
3. Do you like to play board games?	Yes / No	Yes / No
4. Do you like in-line skating?	Yes / No	Yes / No
5. Do you like to listen to music?	Yes / No	Yes / No
6. Can you _____ ?	Yes / No	Yes / No
7. Do you like (to) _____ ?	Yes / No	Yes / No

Compare your answers. What do you have in common?

"I can't paint, and Bernard can't, either. We both like board games."

C Complete the sentences with your own information. Then compare answers with a partner.

1. I can't _____ , but I want to learn.
2. I'm not really into _____ . It's not really my thing.
3. I love to _____ !
4. I'm not very good at _____ , but I *am* good at _____ .
5. I don't really enjoy _____ these days. I prefer to _____ .

A I can't dance, but I want to learn.
B Me too!

Before you watch

A Match the words in the two columns. Write the words.

country	sale	1. _country music_
diet	clubs	2. _____
golf	music	3. _____
junk	racket	4. _____
stoop	drink	5. _____
tennis	food	6. _____

B Circle the correct verb form.

1. **I like** / **I'm liking** country music. What about you?
2. I don't feel very well. I think **I get** / **I'm getting** the flu.
3. Hi. **Do you live** / **Are you living** around here, or **do you visit** / **are you visiting**?
4. I don't want any French fries. **I try** / **I'm trying** to lose weight.
5. I usually **go** / **am going** to the gym every day. What about you?
   Do you go / **Are you going** to a gym?
6. Right now, **I study** / **I'm studying** for my final exams next month.

C Complete the chart with the expressions in the box.

Are you into music?
This is a great party.
Nice meeting you.
✓ Are you kidding?
Have a great day.
No way!
Do you live around here?
I'm sorry, I think I need to go.
Wow! Are you serious?

Starting a conversation	Expressing surprise	Ending a conversation
	Are you kidding?	

While you watch

A Check (✓) true or false. Then try to correct the false sentences.

Matt   **Fred**

1. David has a cold.   ☐ True   ☑ False
   David has a fever.
2. Matt likes Liz's CD.   ☐ True   ☐ False
   _____
3. Matt lives far away.   ☐ True   ☐ False
   _____
4. Fred exercises twice a week.   ☐ True   ☐ False
   _____
5. Matt is a good singer.   ☐ True   ☐ False
   _____
6. Fred drinks a lot of coffee.   ☐ True   ☐ False
   _____
7. Liz thinks Fred is an interesting guy.   ☐ True   ☐ False
   _____

B Who does these things? Check (✓) Liz or Fred. Then watch the video and check your answers.

Who . . . ?	Liz	Fred
1. is a good listener	✓	
2. keeps looking at the other person		
3. talks about himself or herself a lot		
4. asks about a salary		
5. smiles a lot		
6. is negative		

While you watch

DVD 7
VHS 05:49
−08:40

C What do they talk about? Check (✓) the correct topics.

Conversation 1: Matt and Liz		Conversation 2: Alex and Fred	
☐ personal appearance	☐ the weather	☐ personal appearance	☐ the weather
☐ where they live	☐ staying healthy	☐ where they live	☐ staying healthy
☐ exercise	☐ music	☐ exercise	☐ music
☐ personal problems	☐ salaries	☐ personal problems	✓ salaries

DVD 8
VHS 06:53
−08:20

D Listen for these sentences. Circle the ones you hear.

1. a. I drink these diet drinks.
   b. I'm drinking these diet drinks.
2. a. I don't do anything right now.
   b. I'm not doing anything right now.
3. a. Do you make a lot of money doing that?
   b. Are you making a lot of money doing that?
4. a. I play the piano.
   b. I'm playing the piano.
5. a. I go to the gym every other day.
   b. I'm going to the gym every other day.
6. a. I eat a lot of junk food.
   b. I'm eating a lot of junk food.

DVD 9
VHS 07:06
−07:52

E Watch the video. Complete the conversations with expressions from the box.

actually cool no way really wow

Alex Well, (1) __actually__ , I'm a personal trainer.

Fred (2) _____ ? Do you make a lot of money doing that?

Alex Uh . . .

....

Matt (3) _____ , I'm a musician, too.

Liz (4) _____ ! What do you play? Or . . . are you a singer?

Matt No. I can't sing at all. I play the piano.

Liz (5) _____ . What kind of music do you play?

Matt Well, I play jazz.

Liz (6) _____ ! And you live nearby. Maybe we can practice together sometime.

Matt Sure. That sounds great.

After you watch

A What did you learn about Matt and Fred? Make notes. Then compare your answers with a partner. Did you remember the same things?

Matt	Fred
lives nearby	*wants to lose weight*

B Choose one of the conversation ideas in the box or use your own ideas. Have a short conversation with a partner.

your home or workplace   a hobby or interest   the weather

A Do you work near here?
B Yes, I do. I work in an office on Second Street.
A Really? I work near Second Street! . . .

C Imagine you are at a party. Write a conversation with a partner. Follow the steps below.

A (Say something about the party.) _____

_____

B (Respond and ask a question.) _____

_____

A (Respond and introduce yourself.) _____

_____

B (Introduce yourself and ask another question.) _____

_____

A (Respond and give more information.) _____

_____

A This is a great party.
B Yeah. David's parties are always fun. . . .

Act 3

Before you watch

A Complete the sentences about the pictures. Use the words in the box.

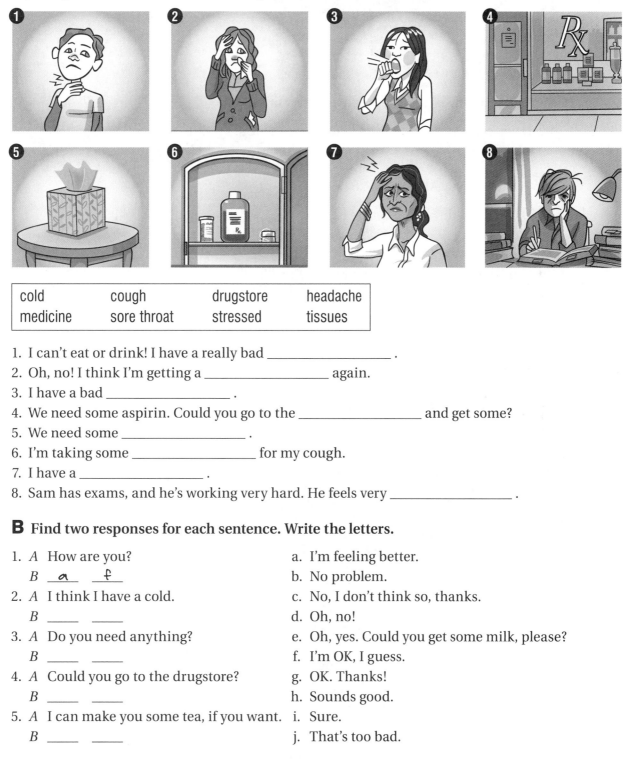

cold	cough	drugstore	headache
medicine	sore throat	stressed	tissues

1. I can't eat or drink! I have a really bad _____ .
2. Oh, no! I think I'm getting a _____ again.
3. I have a bad _____ .
4. We need some aspirin. Could you go to the _____ and get some?
5. We need some _____ .
6. I'm taking some _____ for my cough.
7. I have a _____ .
8. Sam has exams, and he's working very hard. He feels very _____ .

B Find two responses for each sentence. Write the letters.

1. *A* How are you?
   B __a__ __f__
2. *A* I think I have a cold.
   B ____ ____
3. *A* Do you need anything?
   B ____ ____
4. *A* Could you go to the drugstore?
   B ____ ____
5. *A* I can make you some tea, if you want.
   B ____ ____

a. I'm feeling better.
b. No problem.
c. No, I don't think so, thanks.
d. Oh, no!
e. Oh, yes. Could you get some milk, please?
f. I'm OK, I guess.
g. OK. Thanks!
h. Sounds good.
i. Sure.
j. That's too bad.

While you watch

DVD 10
VHS 09:31
−13:36

A Check (✓) all the correct answers.

1. At the beginning of the act, David and Alex talk about _____ .

   ☑ David's health   ☐ David's daily schedule   ☐ the stoop sale
   ☐ Alex's health   ☐ Alex's daily schedule   ☐ David's newspaper article

2. On the telephone, Alex and Yoko talk about _____ .

   ☐ David's health   ☐ Yoko's health   ☐ medicine
   ☐ Alex's health   ☐ Liz's health   ☐ exercise

3. After the telephone call, David and Alex talk about _____ .

   ☐ in-line skates   ☐ a tennis racket
   ☐ skating lessons   ☐ tennis lessons

DVD 11
VHS 09:31
−11:27

B Match the two parts to make true sentences. (One item matches
to two people.)

1. David __e__ ____ ____   a. is coughing a lot.
2. Alex ____ ____   b. has allergies.
3. Yoko ____   c. missed the stoop sale.
4. Liz ____ ____   d. has a cold.
                           e. feels better.
                           f. has a terrible headache.
                           g. is stressed.

Before you watch

A Complete the sentences about the pictures. Use the words in the box.

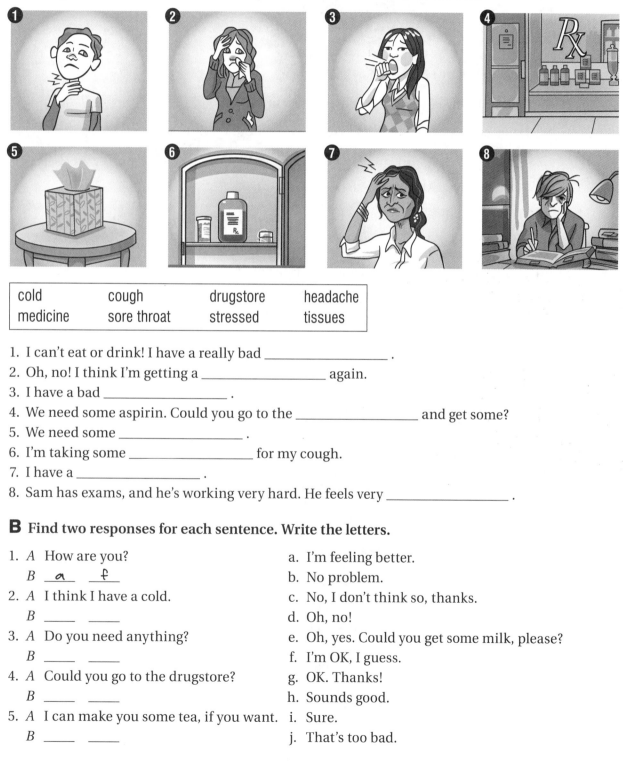

cold	cough	drugstore	headache
medicine	sore throat	stressed	tissues

1. I can't eat or drink! I have a really bad _____ .
2. Oh, no! I think I'm getting a _____ again.
3. I have a bad _____ .
4. We need some aspirin. Could you go to the _____ and get some?
5. We need some _____ .
6. I'm taking some _____ for my cough.
7. I have a _____ .
8. Sam has exams, and he's working very hard. He feels very _____ .

B Find two responses for each sentence. Write the letters.

1. *A* How are you?
   B __a__ __f__
2. *A* I think I have a cold.
   B ____ ____
3. *A* Do you need anything?
   B ____ ____
4. *A* Could you go to the drugstore?
   B ____ ____
5. *A* I can make you some tea, if you want.
   B ____ ____

a. I'm feeling better.
b. No problem.
c. No, I don't think so, thanks.
d. Oh, no!
e. Oh, yes. Could you get some milk, please?
f. I'm OK, I guess.
g. OK. Thanks!
h. Sounds good.
i. Sure.
j. That's too bad.

While you watch

DVD 10
VHS 09:31
−13:36

A Check (✓) all the correct answers.

1. At the beginning of the act, David and Alex talk about _____ .

   ☑ David's health ☐ David's daily schedule ☐ the stoop sale
   ☐ Alex's health   ☐ Alex's daily schedule   ☐ David's newspaper article

2. On the telephone, Alex and Yoko talk about _____ .

   ☐ David's health ☐ Yoko's health ☐ medicine
   ☐ Alex's health   ☐ Liz's health   ☐ exercise

3. After the telephone call, David and Alex talk about _____ .

   ☐ in-line skates   ☐ a tennis racket
   ☐ skating lessons ☐ tennis lessons

DVD 11
VHS 09:31
−11:27

B Match the two parts to make true sentences. (One item matches
to two people.)

1. David __*e*__ ____ ____   a. is coughing a lot.
2. Alex ____ ____   b. has allergies.
3. Yoko ____   c. missed the stoop sale.
4. Liz ____ ____   d. has a cold.
                               e. feels better.
                               f. has a terrible headache.
                               g. is stressed.

While you watch

DVD 12
VHS 09:31
−11:27

C Listen for these parts of the conversation. Circle the correct answers.

1. *Alex*   Hey, David, how are you?

   David   **I feel better.** / **I'm feeling better.**

2. *David*   Oh, no. That's too bad.

   Alex   Yeah. You know, **I get up** / **I'm getting up** at 5:30 every day to go to work these days.

3. *Alex*   What about your article for the newspaper, "A Stoop Sale: Step-by-Step"?

   David   **I want to write** / **I'm still writing** it, but I'm stressed about my deadline.

4. *Yoko*   Hi, Alex. It's Yoko. How are you?

   Alex   OK, I guess. Actually, I think I have a cold. How **do you feel** / **are you feeling**?

5. *Alex*   Really? You're kidding.

   Yoko   No, I'm not. I have cold. And Liz **coughs all the time** / **is coughing a lot**.

DVD 13
VHS 09:31
−13:36

D Who says these things? Check (✓) Alex, David, or Yoko. Then watch the video and check your answers.

	Alex	**David**	**Yoko**
1. I guess it was a 24-hour bug.			
2. We got really wet!			
3. I can go to the drugstore.			
4. You sound sick.			
5. Do you guys have any?			
6. He can buy some.			
7. Now I just have to find my tennis racket.			
8. Sorry! You never used it!			

DVD 14
VHS 12:00
−12:28

E Watch the video. Complete the conversation with verbs from the box.
(Some of the verbs are used twice.)

drink	get	have	rest	take

Alex   No problem. Do you need anything?

Yoko   No, I never take medicine when I (1) _____ have a cold.

Alex   That's funny. I don't either. If I (2) _____ allergies, I usually
(3) _____ something. But when I have a cold, I don't
(4) _____ medicine. I just stay home and (5) _____ .

Yoko   Yeah, me too. But if I (6) _____ a really bad cold,
I (7) _____ hot water and vinegar with honey.

Alex   Really? Does it help?

Yoko   Yeah, it helps a lot.

After you watch

A What can you remember? What does Yoko do when she has a cold? What do you do when you have a cold?

_____

_____

_____

B Answer the questions. Then compare your answers with a partner. How are you the same? How are you different?

	You
1. How often do you get the flu?	
2. How often do you get headaches?	
3. What do you do when you feel sick?	
4. Do you feel stressed a lot?	
5. Do you feel tired very often?	

A   How often do you get the flu?
B   I hardly ever get the flu.
A   Really? You're lucky. I get the flu once a year.

C Work with a partner. Complete the conversations using your own ideas. Then practice with your partner.

1. *A* How are you feeling? Do you still have _____ ?
   B Oh, I'm feeling much better, thanks.
       I _____ and
       now I'm feeling _____ .
   A That's good. I always _____
       when I have a cold.

2. *A* I'm so _____ these days.
   B Really? _____ ?
   A Well, I'm _____ these days.
       And I'm _____ .
   B That's too bad.

Before you watch

A Match the pictures with the sentences.

1. __c__   2. _____   3. _____   4. _____

5. _____   6. _____   7. _____   8. _____

a. He's baking a cake.
b. They're playing soccer.
c. They're making pasta.
d. It's arriving at 5:45.

e. She's leaving work.
f. She's mailing some letters.
g. He's talking on the phone.
h. They're planning a party.

B Are the actions in the conversations happening now, or will they happen in the future? Check (✓) the correct column.

	Now	In the future
1. *A* What are you doing?		
B I'm writing a letter.	☐	☐
2. *A* What are you doing tomorrow?		
B I'm playing basketball with a friend.	☐	☐
3. *A* What are you making for dinner tonight?		
B I'm probably making pasta with chicken.	☐	☐
4. *A* Who are you talking to?		
B I'm talking to my father.	☐	☐

DVD [15]
VHS 13:41
−17:52

A What topics do David, Liz, Yoko, and Alex talk about? Check (✓) one answer for each item.

1. ☐ American stuff
   ☑ Italian stuff

2. ☐ flowers
   ☐ pictures

3. ☐ a special present
   ☐ a special guest

4. ☐ the menu for the party
   ☐ the decorations for the party

5. ☐ a traditional cake
   ☐ a popular dessert

6. ☐ the guest list for the night of the party
   ☐ the plan for the night of the party

7. ☐ a mistake about the date of the party
   ☐ a change in the date of the party

DVD [16]
VHS 13:41
−17:52

B When are these things going to happen? Write the number for each event under the correct day.

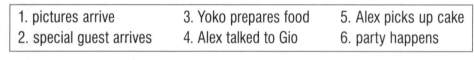

1. pictures arrive   3. Yoko prepares food   5. Alex picks up cake
2. special guest arrives 4. Alex talked to Gio   6. party happens

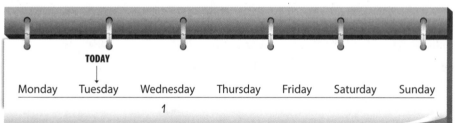

TODAY
↓

Monday	Tuesday	Wednesday	Thursday	Friday	Saturday	Sunday
	1					

DVD [17]
VHS 13:41
−17:52

C Circle the correct answers.

1. Gio isn't **home / homesick**.
2. Gio's **mother / sister** is sending the pictures.
3. Liz is picking up the special guest at the **airport / train station**.
4. Yoko **is / isn't** busy and **can / can't** talk long.
5. Yoko is making pasta, grilled vegetables, and **pizza / hamburgers** for the party.

6. Gio **knows / doesn't know** about the party.
7. Alex **can / can't** bake cakes.
8. Alex **can / can't** keep Gio busy on the night of the party.
9. The party is on the **25th / 26th**.
10. **Liz / David** is going to call everyone back.

While you watch

DVD 18
VHS 13:41
−15:42

D Listen for these sentences. Complete the sentences with the correct form of the verbs in the box. (You will use one of the verbs twice.)

be	love	make	meet	try

1. *David*   He's not ____going to be____ back for another hour.
2. *David*   Gio is pretty homesick, so I think he's _____ all the Italian stuff.
3. *Liz*   And our special guest arrives on Friday morning. I'm _____ her at the airport.
4. *Yoko*   I'm _____ pasta, grilled vegetables, pizza, and stuff like that. I'm excited because I'm _____ some new recipes!
5. *David*   Yoko is _____ pasta and stuff like that.

E Listen for the sentences and complete them with *can* or *could*. Then watch again and match the sentences with the ones that follow them.

DVD 19
VHS 14:56
−16:50

1. It's about the food for the party. __Can__ you tell me what you're going to make? ____
2. I'm preparing a lot of the food on Saturday morning. I _____ talk to Liz about it later. ____
3. So . . . how _____ I help? ____
4. Are you going to bake a cake for him? I _____ help with that. ____
5. It's going to be ready on Friday. _____ you pick it up? ____
6. On the night of the party, we need someone to keep Gio busy. _____ you help? ____

a. Sure. OK. What else?
b. Um, I'm not sure.
c. You know, I make great cakes.
d. Uh, I have to go, OK? Bye, David.
e. Sure. I'm making pasta, grilled vegetables, pizza, and stuff like that.
f. You know what? Gio wants me to train him at the gym.

After you watch

A Think about the plans that were made in the video. What do you think is going to happen on the night of the party? Write your ideas. Then discuss the question.

Alex is going to take Gio to the gym. The others are going to prepare the party.

Who do you think the mystery guest is going to be? _____

B Match the statements with the responses. Then practice the conversations with a partner. Use your own ideas to keep the conversation going.

1. I'm going to a wedding in August. _d_
2. We're going out for dinner this evening. ____
3. We're having a birthday party for my father in July. ____
4. Some friends are coming to visit this weekend. ____
5. I'm going to a concert on Saturday night. ____
6. My sister is graduating this summer. ____

a. Really? Does she have any plans?
b. Oh, yeah? How old is he?
c. I am too! Who are you going to see?
d. Really? Who's getting married?
e. What are you going to do with them?
f. That sounds nice. Are you celebrating something?

C Look at the activities in the box and add two of your own. Then circle three to five activities that you are planning to do sometime in the future.

go to a concert	have a birthday party	go to a wedding
go out for dinner	buy a present	_____
see old friends	go away for the weekend	_____

Work with a partner. Take turns describing your plans. Give details.

A *I'm going away for the weekend.*
B *Really? Where are you going?*
A *Well, . . .*

Episode 2 The Birthday Party

Act 2

Before you watch

A Put the words in the box into the correct categories.

✓ algebra	basketball	classes	costumes	fireworks	float	football
graduation	parade	soccer	subject	uniform	volleyball	

School	Sports	Festivals and celebrations
algebra		

B Complete the sentences with the verbs in the box.

came	got	grew	had	met
moved	took	was	✓ were	wore

1. We ___were___ on the same volleyball team.
2. I _____ up in France, but my family _____ to California when I _____ sixteen.
3. My brother and I _____ along well.
4. He _____ to visit me last year.
   We _____ a great time.
5. I _____ history and geography in high school.
6. Everybody _____ a uniform at my school.
7. My parents _____ in high school.

C Match the questions with the answers. Then practice the conversations.

1. Where were you born? _____
2. Did you play sports when you were a kid? _____
3. Did you get along with your brothers and sisters? _____
4. What was your favorite subject at school? _____
5. Did you study any languages? _____

a. Probably math. I was good at math.
b. Yes, we got along well.
c. In California, but I grew up in New York.
d. Yes, I did. I studied German and Italian.
e. Yes. Volleyball and basketball.

While you watch

DVD [20]
VHS 17:57
−21:19

A Match the sentences with the correct pictures.

a. We did everything together.
b. Is that really you?
c. What are you doing here?
d. Who's that with you?
e. Happy Birthday!
f. I was a good student.

1. _____

2. _____

3. _____

4. _____

5. _____

6. _____

DVD [21]
VHS 20:04
−21:53

B Listen for these topics. Cross out the word in each list that isn't mentioned.

1. Carnevale	2. Sports	3. School subjects
costumes	baseball	algebra
dancing	basketball	business
fireworks	soccer	English
float	volleyball	German
parades		

While you watch

DVD 22
VHS 19:14
–21:36

C Circle all the correct answers. (One, two, or three answers are possible for each question.)

1. Gio and Monica _____ .
   a. had fights when they were kids
   b. went to college together
   c. get along well now

2. Monica came to the party because _____ .
   a. she wanted to surprise Gio
   b. Liz and David invited her
   c. she had vacation time

3. Gio and his cousin _____ .
   a. were in the same classes
   b. played on the same soccer team
   c. grew up in the same house

4. Most students in Gio's school _____ .
   a. spoke English fluently
   b. didn't study hard
   c. studied two languages

DVD 23
VHS 18:34
–19:06

D Complete the conversation.

Gio   Oh my gosh! Where did you get these pictures?

Liz   Your mother (1) __sent__ them to us.

Alex Is that really you? You (2) _____ so little!

Gio   Yeah. I guess I'm three or four months old in that picture. Uh, that (3) _____ probably right before my family moved to Italy.

Kim   Really? You weren't born in Italy?

Gio   No, I (4) _____ here. My mother's a New Yorker. She (5) _____ my father when he (6) _____ to the U.S. to work.

Kim   So (7) _____ you (8) _____ bilingual?

Gio   Not really. We usually (9) _____ Italian at home. My mother speaks it very well.

After you watch

A What can you remember? Read the summary of Gio's life. Find and correct the mistakes.

Gio was born in ~~Italy~~ ^the U.S.. His mother is American and his father is Italian, so the family spoke English at home. He moved to Italy when he was about four years old.

Gio's sister's name is Maria. They didn't get along when they were kids, and they're not really close now. They loved *Carnevale* when they were children. *Carnevale* is a popular festival with parades and fireworks.

Gio and his brother were in the same class at school and on the same baseball team. Gio played a lot of sports as a child.

Gio loved school but he wasn't a very good student. He hated algebra!

B Use the prompts to write questions about your childhood.

1. Where / born   *Where were you born?* _____
2. Where / grow up   _____
3. get along / family   _____
4. Where / go / school   _____
5. What / favorite subject   _____
6. play / any sports   _____
7. What kind / music / listen to   _____
8. What / best memory   _____

C Work with a partner. Choose some of the questions in Exercise B. Take turns asking and answering the questions.

A *Where did you grow up?*
B *Well, I grew up in . . . , but we moved to . . . when I was a teenager.*
A *Really? Did you like . . . ?*
B *. . .*

Act 3

Before you watch

A Match the picture with the correct location expressions.

| a. at the end | b. between | c. on the corner |

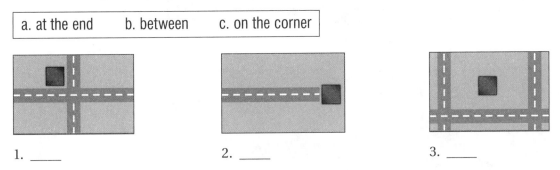

1. _____   2. _____   3. _____

B Look at the map. Write the name of the place for each location.

1. It's at the end of Elm Street. _____

2. It's on Oak Street, between First and Second Avenues. _____

3. It's on Elm Street, between Second and Third Avenues. _____

4. It's on the corner of Elm Street and First Avenue. _____

C Number the lines of the conversations in the correct order.

1. _____ It sounds terrific!

_____ Like what?

_____ Well, there are a lot of nice shops and great restaurants.

_____ Yes, it's great. There's so much to do.

_1_ Do you like living in your neighborhood?

2. _____ OK. Thanks!

_____ I'm sorry? What?

_1_ Excuse me. I'm looking for Luca's.

_____ Oh. That's on Elm Street. It's not far. Go straight ahead for a block. Make a right, and it's at the end of the street.

_____ Luca's Restaurant.

While you watch

A Number the scenes in the correct order.

DVD 24
VHS 22:11
–26:35

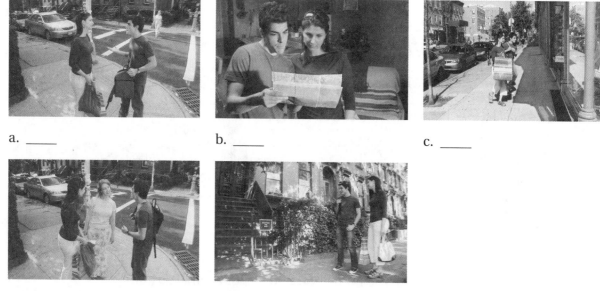

a. _____

b. _____

c. _____

d. _____

e. _____

B What does Gio say is in the neighborhood? Check (✓) yes or no to answer the questions.

DVD 25
VHS 22:28
–24:28

Is there . . . ?			Are there any . . . ?		
1. an aquarium	☐ Yes	☐ No	5. dance clubs	☐ Yes	☐ No
2. a garden	☐ Yes	☐ No	6. department stores	☐ Yes	☐ No
3. a museum	☐ Yes	☐ No	7. gift shops	☐ Yes	☐ No
4. a running path	☐ Yes	☐ No	8. music festivals	☐ Yes	☐ No

C Check (✓) Gio or Monica.

DVD 26
VHS 22:11
–26:35

Who . . . ?	Gio	Monica
1. likes art		
2. has a map		
3. doesn't want to go to the garden		
4. has the idea to go shopping		
5. has to move soon		
6. finds some great stuff		
7. forgets the map		
8. sees a sign for an apartment		

While you watch

DVD [27]
VHS 22:43
−23:59

D Write the names of the places in the correct locations. (You will not label two of the squares.)

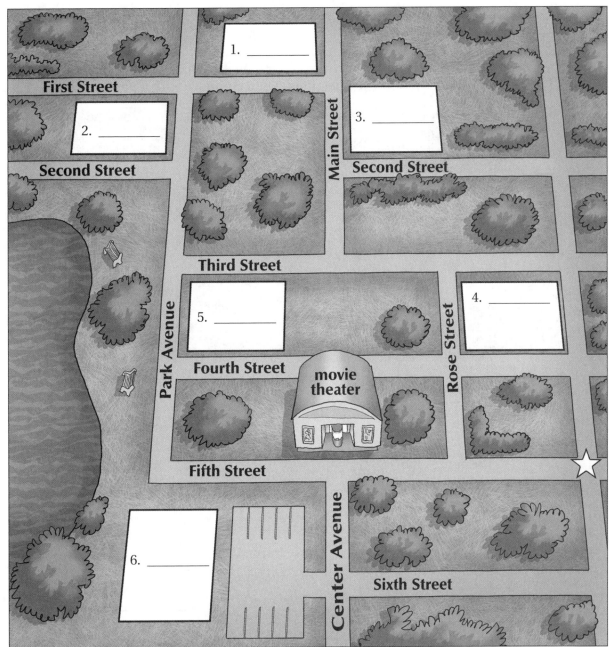

E Circle the correct words to complete the directions.

DVD [28]
VHS 25:46
−26:13

It's **not far** / **pretty far**. The best way to go is: Go straight ahead for **one block** / **two blocks**. You're going to see a **garden** / **movie theater**. Make a **left** / **right** and go down the street for about a block. Take a **left** / **right** and it's at the end of the street. You can't miss it.

Look at the map above. Gio and Monica are at the ☆. Draw the directions.

After you watch

A What can you remember? What's in Gio's neighborhood? What does he like about the neighborhood?

There's a museum and a garden.

B Look at the map. Answer the questions. Then compare with a partner.

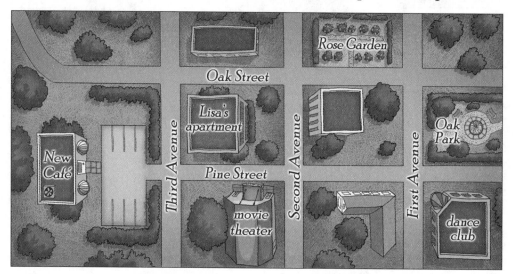

1. Where's the Rose Garden?
   It's on Oak Street, between First and Second Avenues.

2. Where's the movie theater?

3. Where's the dance club?

4. Where's Lisa's apartment?

5. Where's Oak Park?

6. Where's the New Café?

C Work with a partner. Look at the map above and at the map on page 21. These show different parts of the same neighborhood. Choose a place on one of the maps. Tell your partner where you are. Then ask your partner for directions to a different place.

A *Excuse me. I'm looking for the Rose Garden.*
B *Oh, that's on . . .*

How can I use the DVD?

For Video use (General)

To play the Video from beginning to end:
- Select **Play All** on the Main Menu.

To play one Episode of the Video:
- On the Main Menu, select **Episode Menu**.
- On the Episode Menu, select the appropriate **Play Episode**.

To play one Act of the Video:
- On the Main Menu, select **Episode Menu**.
- On the Episode Menu, select **Act Menu**.
- On the Act Menu, select the appropriate **Play Act**.

To play the Video with subtitles:
- On the Main Menu, Episode Menu, or Act Menu, select **Subtitles**.
- On the Subtitles Menu, select **Subtitles on**. The DVD will then automatically take you back to the menu you were on before.

To cancel the subtitles:
- On the Main Menu, Episode Menu, or Act Menu, select **Subtitles**.
- On the Subtitles Menu, select **Subtitles off**. The DVD will then automatically take you back to the menu you were on before.

For Video Activity Pages (VAP) use

If you have watched one Episode/Act of the Video and you want to complete the corresponding exercises in the VAP:
- On the Episode Menu or Act Menu, select **Video Resource Book (VRB) Task Menu**.
- On the VRB Task Menu, select the appropriate exercise. The DVD plays only the section of the Video that students will need to complete that particular exercise. Once the section of the Video has been played, the DVD will automatically return to the VRB Task Menu so that you can make another selection.

If you want to do the relevant exercises without watching the Video (you may have watched the Video at home or in the previous class):
- On the Main Menu, select **Video Resource Book (VRB) Task Menu**.
- On the VRB Task Menu, select the appropriate number. Each number corresponds to a numbered exercise on the **While you watch** pages in the VAP. As above, the DVD plays only the section of the Video that you will need to complete that particular exercise, and the DVD will immediately return to the VRB Task Menu so that you can make another selection.

How can I use the Self-study Audio CD/CD-ROM?

You can use it in two ways: **1** as an Audio CD or **2** as a CD-ROM. Just follow the instructions below. With a CD player, you can listen to the two parts of the conversation from the Conversation Strategy section and complete the Self-study listening exercise at the back of the Student's Book. You can practice the conversation by pausing your CD player. You can do the same listening practice with a computer. You can also practice the conversation, record it, and listen to it. In addition, you can find a list of all the words and expressions from the book. You can add your own vocabulary to the list and organize the words in different ways.

1 Play the disc on an Audio CD player for extra listening and speaking practice.

LISTEN

A Go to the Self-study Listening pages at the back of your book. These pages give CD track numbers, listening exercises, listening scripts, and answer keys.

B Play the conversation from the Conversation Strategy section of the unit (Part 1). Read the conversation as you listen, or listen with your book closed.

C Play the rest of the conversation (Part 2), and do the exercise as you listen. Use the Self-study Listening Answer Key to check your answers.

D Listen to the rest of the conversation (Part 2) again as you read the Self-study Listening Script.

PRACTICE

Practice each line of the conversation. Play Part 1 and Part 2 of the conversation again. Press **Pause** to practice a sentence or line. Then press **Play** and continue. You can read the conversation as you practice or practice with your book closed.

2 Put the disc into a computer for extra practice with listening, speaking, and vocabulary.

LISTEN

A Listen to Part 1 of the conversation. Click on **Listen / Part 1**. Then click on **Play**. You can read as you listen or "Hide" the conversation.

B Listen to Part 2 of the conversation, and do a listening exercise. Click on **Play** and do the exercise as you listen. "Check" your answers. Then listen to Part 2 again. This time you can read the script or "Hide" the conversation.

C Listen to Part 1 and Part 2. You can read the conversation as you listen or "Hide" it.

PRACTICE

Practice each line of the conversation. Click on **Practice** for Part 1 or Part 2. Click on a line to play it. Click on **Record**, say the line, and click on **Stop**. Then "Compare" your line to the original recording.

PLAY A ROLE

Play a role in the conversation. Click on **Play a role** for Part 1, Part 2, or the entire conversation. "Choose" a role. Decide if you want to read your lines or "Hide" them. Then click on **Start**. When it's your turn, click on **Record**, say your line, and click on **Stop**. At the end of the conversation, "Play" your recording.

MY VOCABULARY NOTEBOOK

A Find words and expressions from the Student's Book. Click on **My vocabulary notebook**. Search for the vocabulary in a unit, grammar category, or topic / functional category.

B Write your own notes or example sentences to help you learn new vocabulary. Just click on a specific word or expression, and complete a chart for it.

C Add your own vocabulary to the notebook. Click on **Add word or expression**. You can put your words in categories and write notes and example sentences for them.

D Print useful vocabulary lists. Search for a category of vocabulary, and print the list.

PC
Pentium II; Windows® 98SE or higher; 128 MB RAM; 64 MB available hard-drive space; 8x CD-ROM drive; Mouse; Monitor with thousands of colors and 800x600 screen; 8-bit sound card

Mac®
for Macintosh®; System 8.6 or 9.x or higher; 128 MB RAM; 64 MB available hard-drive space; 8x CD-ROM drive; Mouse; Monitor with thousands of colors and 800x600 screen